DAY OF THE DIESELS
Volume 1: 1970-74

DAY OF THE DIESELS
Volume 1: 1970-74

John Spencer Gilks

Edited by Mike Esau

· RAILWAY HERITAGE ·
from
The NOSTALGIA Collection

First published in 2005

British Library Cataloguing in Publication Data

A catalogue record for this book is available from the British Library.

ISBN 1 85794 240 X

Silver Link Publishing Ltd
The Trundle
Ringstead Road
Great Addington
Kettering
Northants NN14 4BW

Tel/Fax: 01536 330588
email: sales@nostalgiacollection.com
Website: www.nostalgiacollection.com

The number appended to each caption is the negative number. Requests for prints may be made via the Publishers.

Printed and bound in Great Britain

Half title Hurst Green Junction, Surrey; Class 33, commuter train from London Bridge to Uckfield, 14 August 1973.
By this time an hourly service of DEMUs from London to East Grinstead with connection at Oxted to Edenbridge and Uckfield had become standard practice, but this had to be augmented during peak hours and two sets of locomotive-hauled stock were retained, one to serve each line. Until 1955 the two routes came together again at Culver Junction on the approach to Lewes and you could travel from London to Brighton one way and come back the other! There was also a regular service to Eastbourne via Edenbridge. The preserved Bluebell Railway is based on part on the section that closed south of East Grinstead on the day of a railway strike in 1955; south of Uckfield survived until 1969. *107*

Page 2 Calstock, Cornwall (as seen from the Devon side of the River Tamar); DMU, Gunnislake-Plymouth, 14 September 1974.
Prior to 1966 the service originated 5 miles further north at Callington and terminated at Bere Alston, where it connected with the former Southern main line from Waterloo to Plymouth. In its turn this closed here in 1968 and it was thought that the branch would also be doomed. But no! Significant numbers of upmarket commuters guaranteed its survival; indeed, they now had a through service with reversal at Bere Alston. Because of the hilly terrain the line retains height over Calstock Viaduct, 120 feet above water level (and 333 yards long), and hugs the hillside above the community. *1264*

Title page Woolston, Hampshire; DEMU, Southampton-Portsmouth, 16 November 1974.
If you look carefully you can see the bridge being built over the River Itchen that replaced the ageing ferry soon afterwards. To avoid a major river crossing the railway leaves the main line from Waterloo at St Denys and follows a horse-shoe alignment. Currently services are provided regularly this way not only to Portsmouth but also to London via Horsham, and places like Brighton, Littlehampton and Worthing via the curve between Cosham and Havant, which saw few trains prior to electrification. *643*

Left 'The Great Stone of Fourstones' south of Bentham, North Yorkshire; John Spencer Gilks, 15 May 1974.
One of my favourite railways links Settle Junction and Wennington where in the past the trains from Leeds/Bradford were divided with portions running to Morecambe via Lancaster (Green Ayre) or Carnforth. For years I stayed at Close House, Giggleswick, where the line ran through the grounds. Although it survives, the Settle Bypass now runs between the house and the railway and there is peace no longer. I visited this spot between seeing trains on the line. *Photo by Hargreaves*

Right Near Aynho Junction, Oxfordshire; Class 47s, 1V58 Birmingham (New Street)-Paddington via Oxford and equivalent northbound service, 30 March 1974.
Beyond the bridge there used to be water troughs drained by the locomotives of the expresses between Paddington and Birkenhead via Bicester that ran this way until 1967. The spire is at Kings Sutton, served by one of only five stations surviving in Northamptonshire. I am visiting this location by coach in company with members of the 'Talking of Trains' class that I ran in Surbiton from 1960 until 1984 (see earlier books). Today Virgin trains run this way between the North and the South Coast via Birmingham, and Chiltern trains provide an excellent service between the Midlands and Marylebone. *2704*

CONTENTS

Introduction   7

1   South and West   9
2   Wales and the Marches   24
3   Midlands and the North   37
4   The East   70
5   Scotland   108

Index   127

Below Willersey, Hereford & Worcester; Class 47, diverted Newton-le-Willows to Newton Abbot Motorail service, 16 August 1970.
The location is between Honeybourne and Broadway near the home of the Gloucestershire/Warwickshire Railway, which operates from Toddington (see page 42) as far as Cheltenham Racecourse. The preservationists are successors to the BR service via Stratford-upon-Avon, withdrawn in 1967 (locally in 1960). Before then it was common to find regular trains this way from Birmingham (Snow Hill) to Cardiff, and through expresses between Wolverhampton and Weston-super-Mare, and Torquay and Penzance – the latter being 'The Cornishman' with full restaurant car facilities. Why Motorail has been virtually abandoned is a mystery to me. Motorways may have provided quicker road journeys but only for a few years. As I write, caravans have been banned to the slow lane in the Bristol area of the M5 in recognition of the congestion that can only grow everywhere. What better way to travel than dining and sleeping on the train from London, York or elsewhere to Scotland or the West of England with the car behind the coach? The return charge for a car and up to three passengers between Newton-le-Willows and Newton Abbot in 1967 was a maximum of £24! The car carrier here did the out and back journey the same day. *2544*

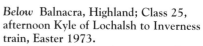

Below Balnacra, Highland; Class 25, afternoon Kyle of Lochalsh to Inverness train, Easter 1973.
The crossing-keeper here spent the time between his few trains as an artist, and what better place could he have chosen for his second career? The road that runs largely parallel to the railway from Garve is no longer so empty at holiday times and the train now is usually a diesel unit. *11025*

INTRODUCTION

Only quite recently have I come to realise that one of the principal reasons I took to rail travel in the 1950s was the availability of space. Usually there was an empty compartment for most of the journey. One could wander up and down the corridor and look out of an open window – supplying fresh air – without bothering other people. While branch-line trains were made up of only one, two or three coaches, others were between eight and a dozen. Later I used to observe the guard walking up and down counting the number of passengers.

The results of these counts must have been analysed by accountants investigating the cost of new trains, some of whom equate them with aircraft. The outcome so often is a DMU in which I feel encapsulated – just enough space for those without long legs and perhaps a seat lined up with a window but by no means always so. I sometimes suffer a degree of claustrophobia and always I am a snob. To be packaged with the herd is not my idea of enjoyment. I worked hard at my exams and in my professional life so as to earn resources to provide a degree of comfort and security. This can no longer be exploited on the train. There is always some apprehension about the running of the service or the behaviour of other passengers. Who will I be obliged to sit next to? And who will have to put up with me? And yet money has not been saved. I'm told that the railway network today costs five times as much to operate as when BR existed.

An attendant providing me with free coffee is no substitute for a proper meal in a dining car. At a time when more and more people are eating out it is a mystery that the dining car is becoming a dying breed. Coupled with the unreasonable and selfish use of the mobile phone by those empty vessels who make the most sound, journeys are no longer fun. I have advised GNER that I will not travel First Class on their trains in future because it is like riding in a telephone exchange. I have a mobile phone for security purposes and incoming calls are only by prior request. I have no wish to become a dog on a lead at anybody's beck and call at any time.

Sadly, therefore, I have to use the car more and more, but it is fortunate that due to lack of local geographical knowledge and inability to read a map accurately most drivers take to the motorways, leaving the secondary roads and country lanes to me.

So I still go to take my railway pictures based on knowledge gained from riding in the train over the years. The prolonged closure of Ipswich Tunnel in 2004 led me to Dullingham, and the sight of lengthy freightliner trains to and from Cardiff (for instance) making their way along the single track between Newmarket and Cambridge was fascinating. The signalman at Dullingham still has to venture from his box – even on the wettest days – to open and shut the level-crossing gates. I understand that to save maintenance costs capstans are to be removed by Network Rail from more 'modern' boxes and sorties to the roadside become more the order of the day. It's called progress! So there is still much of interest out there, but only really in freight trains – the passenger turns all look alike even if the colour of the paintwork changes frequently.

I've been fascinated for years to listen to the rhetoric promoting the transfer of freight from road to rail and to watch what happens in practice. Clearly, as there are so many more voters in cars than lorries, the outcome when the motorways are gridlocked (and without the benefit of railway disciplines) is obvious. Meanwhile I commend readers to turn to Andrew Marr's book *Ruling Britannia* (Michael Joseph, 1995) and to pages 301-314, where he proves that the eclipse of the railways took place during the 1935 general election – just 100 years from the start of the network. One might well ask what railway management and its Parliamentary agents and solicitors were doing to let the road lobby in through the back door. It might be interesting to investigate who they were! I'm a member of the transport livery – The Worshipful Company of Carmen – and I notice that few railwaymen actively participate today whereas road haulage is ever-present. Perhaps it was the same when I was about three years of age.

Consequently *Freightmaster* – the National Railfreight Timetable (published in Swindon) – is at least as important to me now as the National Rail Timetable has always been (though the binding of the May-December 2004 edition of the latter has disintegrated). When this turns up – as mentioned on page 8 of my first book *The Nostalgia of Steam* (Silver Link Publishing, 1994) – I examine which train is provided to familiarise drivers with route knowledge between Old Oak Common, Greenford and Northolt – currently the 8.21pm High Wycombe-Paddington (MF); which uses the spur from Bare Lane to Hest Bank in Lancashire (9.33pm Manchester Airport to Barrow-in-Furness (weekdays); and which connects Stockport (at 2.47pm on Saturdays only) direct with Stalybridge. The 5.50pm King's Cross-Skipton no longer runs via South Milford. The incentive for new services seems to have dried up; the enterprising Norwich-Basingstoke via Brentford and the direct Oxford-Swindon have been discontinued by order of the soon to be redundant Strategic Rail Authority. Railways can never be as flexible as roads, so no new ideas should be stymied so quickly.

While the 'Talking of Trains' WEA evening class at Surbiton (see earlier books) prepares to enter its 44th year under a third lecturer, some adult education colleges are being closed down by county councils who have other priorities for their limited financial resources. The latest of these to my knowledge to close its doors (31 August 2004) is Grantley Hall near Ripon in North Yorkshire. We have had many happy railway weekend courses there in the last 20 years, including two effectively sponsored by Polaroid. Ilford has recently announced redundancies, and I wonder for how much longer I shall be able to acquire slide film and bulbs for my projectors.

On the other hand, a new adult education college has opened in the private sector – Farncombe Estate in the Cotswolds above Broadway in Worcestershire – and I hope to take an active part in its development, not only in recorded music courses but also in railways. If they can make a profit by combining weekend schools with midweek training courses, it suggests that some local authority colleges have not been adequately financed or that imagination is lacking at member and officer level in the Education Department in what can be achieved. Perhaps it is staffing differences that are at the heart of the problem. As with Beeching, however, it's far easier to close down an operation than take positive remedial action.

It may be, of course, that enthusiasts are becoming more elderly as a group. One publisher advises me that the circulation of railway publications is falling, but I can't say I have noticed it in the shops. I've been invited to provide a follow-up to this book covering 1975-79, museums seem to be expanding, and more preserved lines are opening.

Some nuts and bolts to close. The caption to each picture begins with its location (using station names from 1955 and local government areas as in April 1974), then details of the locomotive where known and its train, and the date on which it was taken. The number at the end relates to the colour slide from which the print is produced.

Finally may I close by thanking Peter Townsend for promoting the book, Mike Esau for his editing abilities and patience with me, Will Adams and Mick Sanders for their editorial and layout work for Silver Link, and others for their contributions, especially John Edgington. The logo is designed by Gavin Mist.

John Gilks
Nawton, 2004

Wrenbury, Cheshire; Class 47, Manchester (Piccadilly)-Cardiff Central, and train of steel rods heading north, Easter Sunday, 1970.
It's late March and I'm spending the holiday at All Stretton in White Hart Cottage, the first place at which I stayed away from home in 1956. The two places shared most of the same trains en route through Crewe to South Wales and the West Country. Today the service is much better with hourly trains most of the day and quite a bit of freight. *4051*

1.
SOUTH AND WEST

As I was born and brought up in Kingston-upon-Thames, this area is the one I explored most in the beginning. The annual Sunday School Treat took us by special steam train from Surbiton to Bognor Regis or Littlehampton on the Sussex coast in alternate years. It went via Guildford and Cranleigh (closed 1965) to Christ's Hospital where it reversed and changed engines while an Eldorado ice-cream was given to each of us in the loop-line platform presumably designated for the public school. As a Carman liveryman I now contribute to the school's upkeep through a charity. Consequently the Kingston loop line from Waterloo, the Shepperton branch (where once I inadvertently boarded the 'Ladies Only' compartment at Hampton and hurriedly changed to another at Fulwell), and the 'new' Guildford line via Cobham became the source of regular travels.

While I didn't really care what pulled the coaches, the knowledge that steam traction would be phased out inevitably gave priority to journeys on those lines where it was employed, hence into Kent prior to the 1960 electrification.

I well remember Saturday afternoons (after working in the morning!) when I would join the train from Birkenhead at Guildford at about 2 o'clock and go either to Brighton, Eastbourne and Hastings (in coaches detached at Redhill), or to Folkestone, Dover and Deal for Ramsgate (coaches detached at Ashford), or direct to Ramsgate and perhaps Margate via Canterbury West, on which train a refreshment car was provided. Whenever I went to Ramsgate I returned to London direct on 'The Kentish Belle' (formerly 'Thanet Belle' from 1948) at 6.15pm (having paid a First Class supplement of 3s 6d, or 2s 0d Second), reaching Victoria with four intermediate stops at 8.20pm and taking dinner en route. This was rudely interrupted on one occasion when some of the Pullmans parted with the main train somewhere between Birchington and Herne Bay and we came to a standstill; eventually we were towed back to Margate and set out again on an ordinary train. Pullmans ended regular service

by the time of the Kent electrification, but the diesel service between Redhill and Guildford has greatly improved. The Railway Enthusiasts' Club chartered a two-coach special from Guildford behind a 'USA' tank one evening in connection with a dinner at Deepdene. The train ran as empty coaching stock to Redhill for servicing. What a joy that journey was in the late evening – simple pleasures now denied to us.

Sometimes I would leave the ex-Birkenhead train at Bexhill and walk over to the terminus station known as Bexhill West where a two-coach steam train would push or pull us to Crowhurst on the Tonbridge route from Hastings to Charing Cross. This junction in the woods was so well laid out for passengers that the branch train stopped in a bay on the other side of the up platform from the London express. When this had gone it would shunt over to the equivalent bay on the down side so that Bexhill passengers had the benefit of a similar flat interchange – no need to negotiate the steps of a footbridge or subway here. Everything was correct and the branch was duly shut (1964).

One of my first ventures west on the Southern was in 1952 when, as a National Service airman, I attended a course on religious knowledge at Sidmouth. I had to give a talk about Mary Baker Eddy and the virtues of the Christian Science movement. There seemed an endless succession of junctions west of Salisbury – Templecombe, Yeovil, Chard (closed in 1966 but retained as a loop), Axminster (losing its junction status in 1965), and Seaton (closed in 1966), until ultimately Sidmouth Junction was reached and I joined the branch train through Ottery St Mary and Tipton St John. Here the Exmouth trains diverged, and a year or two earlier I had stayed in a railway camping coach (of LSWR origin) at Newton Poppleford. I took my bicycle with me but at that time it lacked gears and as Devon is famed for its steep hills I was restricted to the valley if I wished to remain in the saddle! The year 1967 saw the loss of the junction and its branch lines.

Probably Midhurst in Sussex was my happiest early railway hunting ground. The line south to Chichester had lost its passenger service as long ago as 1935, but goods survived until 1953 when a culvert gave way and plunged its loco into the mud. The engine was retrieved but the railway was abandoned north of Lavant. Thus I came to walk the rusty track from Cocking station to the mouth of the first long tunnel under the South Downs. I peered into it, saw daylight at the far end, but ventured no further. A Southdown bus on the nearby parallel main road took us round the obstacle to Singleton, where we came upon the two island platforms that had served the crowds to Goodwood race meetings and the fine avenue of trees that led to the station from the main road. This early exploration of a derelict railway undoubtedly created the fascination that has led to a lifelong interest in the subject. Later – with an authorised track permit from the Southern Region – I walked from Elsted to Rogate (closed in 1955) along the track and really enjoyed a glass of beer in the pub there to wash down the dust that I had picked up between the trains. We then travelled to Petersfield (on the train from Pulborough via Midhurst) and the Portsmouth Direct back to Surbiton.

The first of our railtours – three men in a train with a circular tour ticket, aiming eventually to cover the whole BR network as it was in the 1950s – was in the South and West. On 2 April 1956 I caught the 7.43am from Surbiton, joined the four coaches that at Woking (where Alan joined me) were sent to Alton in Hampshire, with Harry getting in at Farnham. We followed what is now known as the Watercress Line (closed by BR in 1973) to Winchester and Eastleigh. Here we took the train for Newbury over the Didcot, Newbury & Southampton Railway (closed thereabouts in 1960/63). Then we went up the branch to Lambourn (closed 1960) and back. On returning to Newbury we joined the Bristol train through Devizes (closed 1966) as far as Holt Junction. Here we travelled north through Melksham to Chippenham, then another return trip over the branch line to Calne (closed 1965). Finally we boarded the express to Swindon and Reading, where we parted company. We had hoped to use a slip coach on the Paddington train, but as it was a Bank Holiday Monday the whole train called at Reading.

Our 16th tour – 25/26 May 1958 – did not go smoothly. We took the sleeper from Paddington to Chacewater (closed 1964), then a junction for Newquay, and had breakfast in the resort. The train from there down the other branch to Par made a tight connection, so I had written to the station master advising him of the situation. As we drew in, the main-line train drew out! Our intention had been to go just to Bodmin Road and thence to Padstow, Bude and Okehampton. In the event, because no train called at both Par and Bodmin Road for hours, we had to journey to Plymouth (with a curry lunch) and go home direct by the Southern route – very annoying, and an appropriate letter of complaint was sent to Paddington. Later we received profuse apologies.

I hope you will enjoy the pictures illustrating the South and West, beginning at Hurst Green near Oxted in Surrey and ending in Cornwall.

Left **Wilton, Wiltshire; Class 47, Cardiff-Portsmouth, 19 August 1972.**
This was a really glorious sunny day in the Wylye Valley, which links Warminster with Salisbury. I make no excuse for reproducing five pictures taken that day; they run from east to west (and there's a sixth in the colour section). I also have happy memories of cycling up the valley in 1955 just prior to the closure of all the intermediate stations. Why I didn't cycle down the valley I don't know! This is a very fertile agricultural area and the crop that has just been harvested has left the fields really golden in colour. The reporting number, 1068, would be from the Southern Region. *1034*

Above **Hanging Langford, Wiltshire; DMU, Salisbury-Westbury, 19 August 1972.**
Some of the brickwork on the bridge has just been replaced – it dates from 1857 when the Wilts, Somerset & Weymouth Railway was opened to Salisbury and Weymouth – and the undergrowth seems to be taking over! It's nice to see overhead telephone wires still in position. *1042*

Right **Wylye, Wiltshire; Class 35 'Hymek', Bristol-Portsmouth, 19 August 1972.**
I'm on a hillside just west of Hanging Langford now, and the chalk downland is much in evidence. There is basically an hourly service on this line nowadays but the trains are no longer made up to eight or more coaches. Currently there is a morning train this way from Carmarthen to Waterloo; when first introduced following privatisation this did not call at Salisbury. Again, the reporting number, 1067, is from the Southern Region. *1044*

Above Heytesbury, Wiltshire; Class 33, Swansea-Bournemouth Summer Saturday extra train, 19 August 1972.

This train comprises maroon coaches, others in blue and white – a scratch set made up for this duty. By this date BR was already running out of spare sets following the Beeching economies. Until 1964 this train had run via Fordingbridge and entered Bournemouth from the west, then continuing to terminate at New Milton because there was no room at the resort. A picture of this working in steam days, approaching Downton Tunnel, appears on page 133 of *The Nostalgia of Steam* (Silver Link Publishing, 1994 & 2001). *1052*

Below Norton Bavant, Wiltshire; Class 35 'Hymek', Portsmouth-Bristol, 19 August 1972.

There are numerous bridges over the railway in quick succession in this area and most are readily accessible to photographers. The joy of these five pictures is that you can go and take them today showing the latest trains and liveries! In this case the reporting number, 1V32, was from the Western Region. *1053*

Opposite above **Cowley Bridge Junction, Devon; DMU, Exeter Central-Barnstaple, 26 September 1974.**
We're on the other side of Exeter St David's now (where Southern trains run south to London while Western trains run north) and have rejoined former LSWR metals. The single-track section in the distance was brought about by the need to reconstruct a bridge over the River Exe following severe flooding. Expresses used to run this way from Waterloo to Plymouth and along the branches to Padstow, Bude, Torrington and Ilfracombe until Stanley Raymond became General Manager of the Western Region and sought to remove all competition to his empire, depriving much of North Devon of direct access to London. Now the 'Tarka Line' to Barnstaple is all that remains, although double track to Crediton does facilitate seasonal services to Okehampton and access to Meldon Quarry for railway ballast. *1164*

Opposite below **King's Nympton, Devon; DMU, Ilfracombe-Exeter Central, 13 June 1970.**
I'm spending the weekend at the Combe House Hotel, Holford, in the Quantocks, and have come over the hills to see trains on the Barnstaple-Exeter line. There is now no loop here nor a LSWR lower-quadrant signal. A train of this length, too, would be unusual. *1173*

Right **Chapelton, Devon; DMU, Ilfracombe-Exeter Central, 13 June 1970.**
I have really nothing to say about this picture, so why do so? *1177*

Below **Bere Ferrers, Devon; DMU, Plymouth-Gunnislake, 14 September 1974.**
I referred above to the story of this service (page 2). This station was served by local trains between Exeter and Plymouth until 1968. The village is situated at the south end of a peninsula between the rivers Tamar and Tavy. It is just over 7 miles to Plymouth by rail; to go by road – and very narrow lanes at that – it is necessary to head in precisely the wrong direction for many miles before turning east then south again. No wonder it was considered impossible to replace the train service. An ageing long metal viaduct over the River Tavy must sometimes cause some anxious moments to the engineers and thoughts of the cost of replacement. When I last saw it only some spans had been repainted and at a distance it looked very peculiar. *1266*

Above left Newbury, Berkshire; special DMU from Welford Park to mark total closure of Lambourn branch, autumn 1973.

I'm just west of the station on the former Great Western main line from Paddington to the West of England. The DMU is standing at the exit from the former branch line to Lambourn (closed 1960 but retained for military purposes as far as Welford Park where it connected with a new siding that ran alongside the M4). I think it is a cold November morning but my diary is not helpful. *1664*

Left Welford Park, Berkshire; DMU, LCGB 'The Isis' special, winter 1970.

Here we are at the post-1960 terminus itself, and the footsteps in the snow indicate that others have been as bold as myself in combating the elements. I think it must be 31 January but the diary is vague. The train took us to Witney on the same day, as I have a photo there and at Eynsham. The film was not developed until April! *1672*

Above Kintbury, Berkshire; Class 52, Paddington-West Country express, 23 June 1973

Look at the mighty telephone poles, and the Kennet & Avon Canal in some dereliction on the extreme right. The railway people were responsible in part for this neglect – why in the UK we cannot let live I don't know. The train destroyed the stage coach, the railways belittled the canals, and now the highways have excessive priority. Competition is the 'in' word, but co-ordination and co-operation between modes would be much more helpful to the consumer. *1680*

Below Witham (site of station), Somerset; Class 45, up aggregate train, 16 September 1974.

This train marks the earliest days of the massive aggregate traffic that now originates in the hills near Frome under the auspices of Foster Yeoman and is brought to building sites in London and the Home Counties every weekday. Until 1963 a passenger service left Witham for Shepton Mallet, Wells and Axbridge, and rejoined the main network (the Bristol & Exeter line) at Yatton. Access can still be gained to the East Somerset Railway. *1740*

Bicknoller, Somerset; Class 35 'Hymek', 1C17 Paddington-Minehead through Saturday train, 13 June 1970.
The branch closed in 1971 but was re-opened five years later by the West Somerset Railway, which continues to thrive. On its return journey this train is illustrated in colour at Williton on page III of *Dawn of the Diesels Part 3* (Silver Link Publishing, 2003). *1774*

Above Dunster, Somerset; DMU, Taunton-Minehead, 13 June 1970.
We remain on the branch to illustrate a typical local train in the year before BR closure. *1783*

Below Doniford, Somerset; DMU, Minehead-Taunton, 13 June 1970.
One of the most scenic spots on the branch – which can still be photographed – is between Williton and Watchet where the track skirts the sea at Bridgwater Bay. *1780*

Below Cowley Bridge Junction, Devon; Class 25, special working of empty hoppers, 26 September 1974.
This train will reverse in the yard at Exeter St David's, then head for Meldon Quarry. In so doing it will use the single line diverging to the left, seen also on page 16. *1809*

Bottom Cowley Bridge Loop, Devon; Class 45, 1E37 Paignton-Bradford (Forster Square), 26 September 1974.
I've crossed the road from the picture above to see this express – a real train of at least 11 coaches. It's the successor to 'The Devonian', which was akin to 'The Cornishman' mentioned earlier on page 6. *1810*

Right Teignmouth, Devon; Class 45, 1E37 Paignton-Bradford (Forster Square), 24 March 1973.
This is the same train the previous year. I wonder who it is that is waving so vigorously at me? The train has just entered the famous coastal section running through Dawlish, which proved so disastrous for the new Virgin trains when they were introduced to high seas. *1848*

Below right Combe St Stephen Viaduct, Cornwall; Class 52, Penzance-Paddington express, 29 September 1974.
I'm told that a crowd of railway photographers gathered in this field some years ago to witness an up special. They had not sought the landowner's permission to be there and when he showed up he was not best pleased. But his attitude changed when one of the group explained that he had come from as far as the North of England to take this picture and perhaps £1 per head might be acceptable. The farmer returned home far better off than when he arrived! This viaduct is on the section between Burngullow and Probus, which was singled and is now being restored to double-track. How much did this economy cost? *2007*

2.
WALES AND THE MARCHES

On an occasion when I flew back from the Isle of Man to Heathrow in the early evening I was intrigued to notice from the street lighting patterns that the South Wales valleys slope from east to south-west beyond Swansea and are then predominantly from north to south-east to Cardiff and Newport. The mass of railways in these valleys has been drastically pruned since the loss of the coal industry and consequent unnecessary duplication; it was common for one company to run its tracks up one side of a valley and another on the opposite side, and by the time the Barry Railway was built in the 1880s it had to go over viaducts across the valleys and through tunnels into the next!

We travelled in some style to Carmarthen on 25 April 1970. The 'Talking of Trains' class had enjoyed at least one annual special charter for three years and I thought that it was time to spread our wings further. West Wales is quite a long way from Surbiton, so I enquired whether we could hire a Blue Pullman set, which would be spare on a Saturday, to add to our comfort. This was agreed for a fee of £1,000, which would include a full breakfast and dinner at the 212 seats. Harry took one of the coaches by way of a factory outing.

Because of the AWS gear under the train it had to avoid the District Line on its way from Old Oak Common, where it was stabled, and went to and fro over the points at Clapham Junction to leave the line from Olympia and gain the main line to Surbiton. It stood in the 'Hampton Court platform' from 6.54 until 7.24am with a Pullman attendant at every door. We left on time, switched to the main line at Hampton Court Junction and called at Woking and Guildford. In order to fill the train we had advertised it in the stock-broker belt as a luxury land cruise.

There were delays in reversing at Guildford so it was fortunate that a member of the class who worked in the Wimbledon HQ had instructed the signalman at Wokingham to give us priority over a train due from Waterloo, which was held at the signal as we passed. Our late arrival at Reading meant that passengers for the Fishguard boat train had to change platforms at the last minute. But by Swindon we were on time until a signal check on the Swansea Avoiding Line near Briton Ferry saw a train of empty coal wagons cross our path from a nearby colliery. The approach to Carmarthen was hindered by works on the line and I found that the amplifier on the Pullman needed 2 minutes to heat up before I could give advice about changing into the DMU, which took us along the 'milk' lines to Felin Fach and Pont Llanio. An old railwayman travelled with us from Bronwydd Arms.

On our return to Carmarthen the smell of cooking turkey encouraged us back to the Pullmans, which changed from the outward route at Patchway and went via Bath to Salisbury to set down at Basingstoke (for Reading) and Woking (for Guildford). The start of engineering works in the Wylye Valley was delayed until we had passed. A real adventure in Wales!

The Swansea Avoiding Line sees few regular trains today. During the summer the lunchtime boat connection at Fishguard has run this way (but next year...?); for four days in July an extra service runs to Builth Road for the Royal Welsh Agricultural Show; otherwise there are two or three freight trains each day. I wanted to photograph one of these – the 2.40pm Margam-Trostre, bearing a load of steel coil – on the viaduct over the A4067 at Morriston north of Swansea. The space between the spans has enabled a dual-carriageway to be built at one level and the old road to be retained higher up adjacent to a significant grassy area. You can see only a small part of the viaduct as the rest to the east is hidden by trees. I took up my position, camera in hand, looking like a lemon and all ears above the traffic trying to identify the train. I anticipated a quick crossing without much warning. In the event a 10mph speed limit had been imposed on the viaduct and the train crawled into view enabling two good pictures to be obtained. In view of its reduced speed, it occurred to me that I could overtake it on the nearby M4 and see it again at, say, Llangennech. A man sitting on a seat there advised that the train had not yet passed. Soon afterwards I photographed it at some speed passing the halt. It transpired that the gentleman had bought one of the *Dawn of the Diesels* volumes, so we had a lot in common. If you live long enough, more people will get to know your name! He was not like the fellow at Cark station in Cumbria who recently advised me that a nuclear flask train had passed when it hadn't, and I was to see it from my moving car minutes later. Perhaps he thought I was a terrorist.

The lunchtime Fishguard boat train – one of only two trains regularly to traverse the branch from Clarbeston Road – has always been a must for photography in the area. Behind its Class 37 I have snapped it at Bridgend, near Jersey Marine, emerging from Lonlas Tunnel (when it proved to be a DMU as the loco had gone to Builth Road), near Waungron, Burry Port, Kidwelly, Clunderwen (two locations), and Fishguard itself when I travelled on the train. I also photographed it when formed by an HST at Clarbeston Road, emerging from Spittal Tunnel and Clunderwen. These pictures are only in recent years, and there are two on the branch in 1970 in this chapter. A farmer has been obliging on two occasions, letting me reach a location above Letterston Junction.

The Cambrian has always provided scenic locations for pictures, although there is only one in this book. I was sorry to see the end of freight on the line when the oil tank train from Aberystwyth was withdrawn. I managed to capture this from the bird sanctuary near Glandyfi looking across the Dovey estuary. The short-lived steam working between Machynlleth and Pwllheli provided another happy sight in later years. I chartered the saloon at the rear of the train with a friend; he had half for his party and I had the other, both with buffet lunches. It so happened that the northbound journey was in rain. We insisted that the saloon should be uncoupled and placed again at the back of the train in Pwllheli. My friends were lucky enough to have glorious sunshine for the return leg and we looked out at the mountains to the north and across the sea to the west. Why aren't such opportunities available now?

One of our railtours in Wales took us from Paddington by sleeper to Neath. Here we joined the 7.40am to Hirwaun and the 8.21 through the tunnel (shored up on both sides and in the roof!) to Merthyr Tydfil. After a leisurely breakfast we took the bus up to Dowlais (Cae Harris) station and the 11.32 to Nelson & Llancaiach, then to Quaker's Yard (High Level); by walking to the Low Level station we gained Cardiff and returned home.

I hope you will enjoy the pictures, which take you from Church Stretton to Wye Valley Junction near Chepstow via the Central Wales Line.

Church Stretton, Salop; DMU, Crewe-Cardiff, 28 September 1974.
We start with a number of scenes now on the line between Shrewsbury and Newport (Gwent). This used to carry several expresses each day between Liverpool/Manchester and the West of England via the Severn Tunnel, but it was downgraded during the Beeching era and the trains were re-routed via Birmingham in the belief that there would be more demand that way and economies could be made. In practice the service along the Marches has improved notably and there is now a basic hourly series of passenger trains this way (DMUs) and they make more wayside stops than hitherto. There is a southbound loop at Church Stretton and the tracks are shared as far as Craven Arms with the Central Wales service, which we shall see later. *2854*

Ludlow, Salop; Class 47, West Country-North West express (1A89), 28 March 1970.

This is a town that has seen a vast improvement in its stopping train service. At the time of this picture hardly anything called there, but now there is something most hours linking the community with Shrewsbury and Hereford. Do notice the vast array of telephone wires and the height of the supporting poles. The goods shed has survived but is no longer rail-connected. The Class 47, in green livery, has emerged from the tunnel to pass northwards through the station; the stock is Mark 1 coaches from the 1950s, now seen only on preservation lines. *2900/2899*

Above Ludford, Salop; Class 45, West Country-Manchester (Piccadilly) Summer Saturday extra (1M93), 5 August 1972.
From the tunnel at Ludlow the line soon enters some hilly country as it heads south, with the bypass to its east. Clee Hill dominates the horizon behind me; it used to boast an inclined plane to bring mineral traffic down to the railway just north of Ludlow. *2901*

Below Orleton, Hereford & Worcester; Class 45, Manchester-West Country Summer Saturday extra (1V42), 5 August 1972.
Since our last picture we have passed through Woofferton, junction for Tenbury Wells and Bewdley until 1961. A one-coach push-pull unit with an 0-4-2T used to operate a service from Ludlow to Tenbury Wells and Leominster and return; on Bank Holidays the late afternoon train from Tenbury would be extended to Kidderminster. When we used this I had written to the station master there asking him to be good enough to ensure that it connected with the Paddington coaches of a train from Stourbridge Junction. Our train was held on the branch and we feared the worst. But in the event we were brought into the platform behind another train – an unusual event in those days – and a loudspeaker announcement asked us to hurry over the bridge where the express was waiting. A porter held open the door to a First Class compartment – obviously it was assumed that someone who wrote such letters travelled First Class! Our two coaches were added to the main train at Worcester (Shrub Hill) and we enjoyed dinner en route to London. *2909*

Leominster, Hereford & Worcester; Class 47, Manchester-West Country express (1V75), 28 March 1970.
Do notice the vast empty area where sidings formerly existed for exchange traffic with the branches to Bromyard/Worcester (closed 1952/1964) and to New Radnor (closed 1951/55 – do you recall the elephant in Bertram Mills Circus who travelled backwards from Leominster and died at Kington?). There is now a loudspeaker system at this station with a mystery voice advising of late running of trains. 2911

Right **Abergavenny, Gwent; DMU, Crewe-Cardiff, 27 October 1973.**
When the line was downgraded, BR was obliged to add an extra single car to the sets so as to maintain an acceptable speed and to provide buffet cars on most journeys. The civil servant responsible for overseeing the implementation of such conditions travelled from Crewe on one occasion only to find no extra unit and no buffet, and that according to other passengers the latter was not uncommon. Because the train could not keep to schedule his connection was missed at Newport and he phoned the relevant General Manager to remonstrate with him. Such attention to detail resulted in transfer to another post. There is now a bypass immediately behind the building on the right. *2948*

Below **Nant-y-Derry, Gwent; Class 25, early afternoon Crewe-Cardiff train, date uncertain.**
I wonder whether this picture should be in the book! Do notice the characteristic Great Western location of the signal on the wrong side, as it were, to assist sighting. The box has now gone so the problem doesn't arise. The track looks so new that rust is prevalent. This is the last picture on the Marches line. *2954*

Left **Glynneuadd, Dyfed; Class 35 'Hymek', Pont Llanio-Carmarthen milk tanks, 24 May 1970.**

The partner to this picture (wrongly numbered!) appeared in *Dawn of the Diesels Part 1* (Silver Link Publishing, 1998) and details of how it was obtained appeared on page 32. The location is between Llanpumpsaint and Pencader stations, both closed in 1965, which resulted in the loss of an internal network of lines from South to North Wales and no doubt contributed to the rise of nationalism. Whereas it had been possible to travel from Carmarthen to Aberystwyth within the principality, now it is necessary to go via Shrewsbury, yet there is still much trumpeting about the inferior substitute service (05.43 Holyhead-Cardiff and 17.14 return on weekdays with an equivalent Sunday working). *3104*

Left **Wolf's Castle, Dyfed; Class 47, 16.30 Fishguard & Goodwick-Kensington Olympia Motorail, 23 May 1970.**
The train is crossing the bridge over the Western Cleddau river and is surrounded by gorse in full bloom. The coaches bear destination plates on the sides as on the continent, a practice that didn't last long here. A driver, car and up to three passengers travelled for £33 (First Class) or £27 (Second) return on a Saturday in 1969, with reductions on other days. Meals, drinks and snacks were available, and the set made an out and back trip in the day. We have already discussed the virtual demise of Motorail services above. *3219*

Top **Tregroes Moor, Dyfed; Class 52, Fishguard-Swansea empty stock (5Z95), 23 May 1970.**
In the background can be seen the outskirts of Goodwick. Those were the days when demand necessitated extra trains to the port and BR was able to meet it. Since then the service has been gradually curtailed until in 2004 there was no through service from Paddington. The daytime HST has been replaced by a commuter set from the Welsh

valley at Rhymney making its pilgrimage behind an aging Class 37 locomotive; it is even relegated to wait in a loop between Bridgend and Cardiff on its return run to make way for more important traffic. When I travelled on it last year there was no shortage of enthusiasts to augment the genuine travellers, and the return fare from Bridgend was incredibly cheap. I was able to use the open window of the door on the vintage stock to obtain photographs of Morlais Junction East, which had eluded me on the ground for years. *3232*

Above **Templeton, Dyfed; DMU, Tenby-Whitland, 23 May 1970.**
This is a branch that in my experience lacks much pictorial coverage in the railway press. It is not easily accessible for the first 5 miles through Lampeter Vale, but between Narberth and Pembroke Dock there are plenty of opportunities including the amusing sight of the guard of the 'Pembroke Coast Express' HST from Paddington holding up the train while opening the level-crossing gates at Manorbier at around 2 o'clock on Summer Saturday afternoons. *3151*

Left Sugar Loaf summit, Powys; DMU, Shrewsbury-Swansea, 27 October 1973.
We turn our attention now to the Central Wales Line, which runs as a single track for some 80 miles from Morlais Junction north of Llanelli to Craven Arms on the Marches line, illustrated earlier. Its own route direct to Swansea Victoria from Pontarddulais was closed in 1964. Trains often cross and change crews at Llanwrtyd Wells, a community much loved in the days of the spa towns but now without even a competing bus service. *3291*

Below left Borthddu, Powys; two Class 37s, eastbound special, 20 April 1974.
Unfortunately the weather in the mountains can be quite unpredictable and this special over the Central Wales Line was not blessed with the brightest day. We are standing beside a cattle grid on the lane to Bryn-hynog and have advised a passing farmer that a lamb has fallen through the grating. Railway photography can be quite hazardous! We shall see this train return later at Knucklas (page 34). *3293*

Above right Llanwrtyd Wells, Powys; DMU, Shrewsbury-Swansea, 20 April 1974.
The special has gone eastwards and we are left with the standard service of four trains each way on weekdays and now one each way on Sundays. I recall the Clerk of the former Knighton Rural District Council telling me that he kept a close watch on the postcode for the town. If it changed it meant that the post would no longer come by train and would mark a step on the road to closure. The postcode changed and more mail vans appeared, but the Prince of Wales saw to it that the trains kept running. Indeed, the Royal Train used the route again on 21 July 2004 (according to the lady who runs the petrol station in Bucknell where I filled up) to bring Her Majesty the Queen to the 100th Royal Welsh Show at Builth Wells. She said that all the curtains were drawn and still the same when it returned empty stock from Llandrindod Wells where the monarch took to a helicopter. There could have been a full track occupation there for the annual four-day train must have been due from Cardiff to Builth Road. *3296*

Below Garth, Powys; DMU, Shrewsbury-Swansea, 4 March 1972.
On 30 November 1973 I attended in my professional capacity a conference of Welsh councillors at the Afan Lido, Port Talbot. As usual I illustrated my address with slides and showed this one to the audience in the morning. In the afternoon the then Chief Executive of BR gave his paper and in the subsequent questions a councillor asked him why there were no lights at Garth Halt; he said that it would be dark there now and the timetable advised potential passengers to wave a red light to stop the train, which, he felt, might be misunderstood in other circumstances and was totally unacceptable. In reply the Chief Executive told him that, even in November, he didn't know what grant the Government was likely to award BR in January, so couldn't be sure to invest in lighting at Garth Halt. However, if local government could persuade central government to give BR three-year grants he would install the lights. Within a short time the Ministry was so persuaded and fine columns now illuminate the halt. I shared a compartment back to Reading with the Chief Executive and he chain-smoked all the way; sadly he didn't have much longer to live. *3298*

Left Llangunllo, Powys; Class 37, eastbound Central Wales Line special, 14 October 1972.

On the subject of life, and without wishing to be morbid, by coincidence one of my best friends was in this train when it passed and at almost the same moment his mother died in the South of England; he was to learn the sad news when he left the train. This station and associated cottages reached the depths of dereliction in the years when the future of the line was in the balance; now they are restored and add to the scene. *3320*

Below left Knucklas, Powys; two Class 37s, returning special, 20 April 1974 (see page 32).

This superb viaduct has castellated ends and dominates the area nearby. A footpath crosses the line at the western end, so it is possible to look along the structure and marvel at Victorian engineering; there is not a tie-bar to be seen. The halt that serves the community used to boast a sign declaring that the track was the best in the locality. This is the last of the series of pictures on the Central Wales Line. *3338*

Above Coed-y-Uyn, Gwynedd; DMU, Pwllheli-Machynlleth, 27 May 1970.

I'm standing with my back to Black Rock Sands looking towards the Snowdon range and it's sunny! We are waiting for the weekly freight to return from the coast; on other days it used to terminate at Penrhyndeudraeth with explosives, but when it came it consisted only of an engine and brake-van. *3567*

Right Blaenau Ffestiniog, Gwynedd; DMU from Llandudno, 29 May 1970.

Will this slate soon be carried away by new freight trains on a regular basis, or will the costs of using the branch make rail transit unviable? When the infrastructure had to be restored recently following flooding, it is said that it was made strong enough for the proposed trains. There is no shortage of waste material. The DMU has just emerged from Blaenau Tunnel whose northern portal is located in magnificent scenery (see the colour photograph in *Dawn of the Diesels* Part 3, page XIII (Silver Link Publishing, 2003). *3686*

Wye Valley Junction, Chepstow, Gloucestershire; Class 35, aggregates train, 26 March 1971.
The Class 35 is heading the train of aggregates from the quarry near Tidenham wrong line from the junction with the Gloucester-Chepstow route to the station. No traffic has used the truncated end of the branch to Tintern and Monmouth (closed 1959), which ends in a quarry, for years, although I believe the track is in situ. What its condition is like in the long tunnel into the Wye Valley goodness knows! There has been substantial main-road construction in the vicinity of the junction since this picture was taken, with a new road bridge over the river parallel to Brunel's famous structure. *2287*

Wye Valley Junction, Chepstow, Gloucestershire; Class 45, Cardiff-Birmingham express, 26 March 1971.
This second picture shows the end of the branch used by the freight. It would appear to be quite steep – note the catch points to divert runaway wagons. *2286*

3.
MIDLANDS AND THE NORTH

My favourite railway in this region was the Great Northern/London & North Western Joint Line that ran from Welham Junction on the Rugby-Peterborough line, north-east of Market Harborough, passed Marefield Junction after some 15 miles, for the Leicester (Belgrave Road) branch, and continued for another 15 miles to a station known as Harby & Stathern situated midway between those villages. Here a line diverged towards Nottingham while the main line headed north to pass under and connect with the Grantham line and to join the East Coast Main Line at Newark (Northgate). Local passenger services were withdrawn mainly in 1953, although Cotham had lost its stopping trains in 1939. Summer weekend services continued to run between Leicester and Mablethorpe/Skegness until September 1962.

Why do I like this line so much and continue to visit its remains to this day? It was built to a very high standard across the wonderful undulating country known as High Leicestershire. Just to see it stride away from Welham Junction and head straight for the hills was a tonic. Apart from the Summer weekend trains I knew it only in the days of the occasional freight. The signalman at Marefield Junction told me that one of these would come on line from the south and take anything up to an hour to reach him. He had to be on duty until 4am on a Sunday morning to deal with some service, which seemed ridiculous in the circumstances and expensive. One day I stood near Thorpe Satchville and watched the plume of a southbound freight climb away from Melton Mowbray. It took nearly half an hour to cover 6 miles! The cutting is still there with a farm track at the bottom. Driving north from Hallaton one Friday afternoon I spotted smoke in my rear-view mirror and turned off the road down a track to a point above the tunnel near East Norton. I had plenty of time to park my Morris Minor, stroll through a coppice, with the sound of the train crawling closer, and look down upon it as it emerged into the daylight past a lofty LNWR signal with co-acting arms and another arm for traffic in

the opposite direction midway between the two. The service was so erratic that I must have spent hours beside the track happily enjoying the splendid surroundings. I visited Melton Mowbray North one evening after dinner and there stood a freight while its loco took water before heading out into the night.

I had but one nearly complete journey over the line – on Sunday 2 June 1957 – when the RCTS ran its 'Mercian' tour from Euston to St Pancras, taking in Welham Junction to Nottingham. But it was a real disappointment to me. No stops were made and the driver seemed to want to go at the maximum permitted speed, which led to a long stand at Saxondale Junction awaiting time. What a wasted opportunity! I determined there and then that if I ever had the chance to charter trains these would stop at out-of-the-way stations to let participants take the air and experience the local environment even if for only 10 to 15 minutes. I have been a member of the RCTS (6680) for years and enjoy *The Railway Observer* each month, but I did wonder at the priorities of the then General Secretary in handling tours. He kindly gave an interview to me and a BBC producer on 3 October 1959 on the London River railtour, but was largely incoherent – he just droned on aimlessly – and we had to bin the tape. What a pity! I was able to cover the section from Bottesford to Leicester on a train from Skegness, and from Newark to Bottesford in one of the saloons chartered to the Friends of the National Railway Museum.

Another line that used to fascinate me ran from Market Drayton to Stoke-on-Trent, passing above the West Coast Main Line at Madeley Road (closed 1931) and through the grounds of Keele University. It lost its through passenger service in 1956. My photographs are spread over quite a period: a freight at Norton-in-Hales (1963), a disused but complete station with signals and thickly rusty track (date unknown due to being an Agfa slide) at Pipe Gate, and another freight at Madeley Road (1963). Here the line was cut back from the west and joined by a new chord to the West Coast Main Line. The only way to gain ready access to a site to view the WCML bridge was by permission of a kindly signalman at Madeley Road box in 1967, who allowed us to walk across and take up position in a nearby field. Imagine my delight on 20 May 1998 when I came across a train in the loop there with the loco 'running round'. I then pursued this to Silverdale Colliery, where I had taken an uninspiring picture in 1991. I had covered the line between Stoke and Keele on a special that then headed north to Harecastle via Leycett, which closed to passengers in 1931 and to goods in 1963. My only other encounter was when travelling north on the M6 and seeing an '8F' appear before me heading west over the motorway with coal trucks, but I didn't dare stop!

Buxton is another place where freight trains seem to run to their own timetable. They tend to come in along the valley from Peak Forest, the locomotives run round in sidings adjacent and east of the line to Manchester, and they then head for Harpur Hill along the remains of the route to Ashbourne. I have 'conquered' these by sitting in a layby on the A6 above Wye Dale and, when the train has passed, driving through King Sterndale to wait beside the line near the quarry – two bites at the same cherry.

The Hope Valley is easily accessible from Buxton and this has seen a heyday of traffic this year with the routing that way of the St Pancras-Manchester (Piccadilly) service introduced on a temporary basis to compensate for delays caused by the rebuilding of the West Coast Main Line. This has run virtually every hour on weekdays. I decided to try it from Manchester to Leicester and return soon after it started, using HST sets that seemed to be made up in some cases of coaches from various sources. I was not to know that my journey was to take place on the hottest day of the year. Sadly the air-conditioning was not working in the First Class coach, nor was there a proper buffet car service. We enjoyed the Hope Valley and the Erewash Valley (which normally has few decent trains) but delays ensured a half-hour-late arrival. The return was no better and we missed our connection in Manchester. There is only one significant single-track section on this route – the short west-to-south curve at Dore, avoiding Sheffield – and sure enough the up and down trains were due to meet thereabouts. The signalman at Totley Tunnel East advised me that he accepted the down train first and I saw the up train held while it came off the curve. But it was a joy to photograph such trains in the stunning scenery west of Edale and to notice the procession of passenger and freight trains into which they were channelled passing semaphore signals.

I often stay near Chester, and in 2004 the Euston/Holyhead trains proved the greatest interest. On the section west of Crewe old Class 47 locomotives were brought into service, but in my experience this was not a success. The first day on which I saw the up afternoon train I thought it must be something else as it was 1 hour 45 minutes late. Next day, near Wavendon, I met other photographers who eventually rang Crewe Information Centre to ascertain the same up train's whereabouts. They were informed that it was 2 hours late, which meant that it had only just left Holyhead, and they went home. I hung on and it was indeed as late as reported, preceded by a train of aggregate wagons, which could not have improved its timekeeping.

Chester used to be served by the Cheshire Lines Committee, an offshoot of the Great Central Railway from Marylebone. I miss the latter very much, for I once enjoyed Summer evenings on the North Bucks/Northamptonshire border seeing the steam workings through the wide cuttings and over the vast embankments and hearing them for miles in the quiet countryside. Summer afternoons, too, were wonderful, with extras from the South Coast to the Midlands and the North joining those from the main line at Culworth Junction. I have seen a train held at each signal there simultaneously waiting a path. Will the great freight way from Liverpool to the Channel Tunnel materialise and the track be restored? By virtue of the big-name contractors associated with the venture, I have sufficient faith to believe that it will in my lifetime. At Finmere, where the tracks used to part to enfold the platform, the two bridges survive over the A421 and a single track remains under the vegetation between the former Grendon Junction and Akeman Street. 'Binliner' waste trains continue to use the few miles between Grendon and Calvert – small matters, but a change from the destruction one normally sees.

Eventually trains from Marylebone reached Penistone and Woodhead. Work was taking place in the redundant 'new' tunnel at Dunford Bridge when I last passed there. The surviving line to Huddersfield was part of the Lancashire & Yorkshire Railway empire. Again it sails across the high ground with a succession of tunnels and viaducts that never cease to amaze. The station that was called Shepley & Shelley has now lost the latter part of its name; but Shelley became the Village of the Year 2004, in a competition of which I am proud to be the Yorkshire Chairman.

Another interesting line in our area that has little publicity links Wigan with Southport. From Appley Bridge it runs west almost straight across the moss of north-west Lancashire with fascinating surviving stations at such rural locations as Bescar Lane, New Lane and Hoscar, and these have a number of stopping trains throughout each weekday. I wonder what it is like to get out at Bescar Lane at 10.39pm on a cold winter's night?

The Furness route from Carnforth to Barrow, Millom, Whitehaven and Workington has always fascinated me. It cuts across the rivers Kent and Leven while the main road meanders round, and frequently there are glimpses of the sea and endless reflections in the water. The procession of nuclear flasks to and from Sellafield provides a variation from the inevitable DMUs. At Drigg, during the foot and mouth crisis, a young policeman politely asked me whether I was all right. From his new road barrier and sentry box he had seen me wandering up and down the nearby bridge while the car stood on the adjacent green. I wonder what he would have thought had he known I photographed the nuclear flask train in the cutting. No harm intended – just another picture to add to the collection. I have enjoyed taking photos of freight between Maryport and Carlisle. This is a pleasant stretch of country and during most mornings there is a train of rails from Workington and an Enterprise working with a Q train for the engineer the other way early afternoon. Lunch can be taken in Cockermouth during the interval!

Finally, I must mention the Newcastle-Carlisle line, which also carries regular freight workings during the day. These are a fine sight amidst the rolling hills.

One of our 'three men in a train' railtours linked the Midlands and North with the East section. We left Euston on 30 July 1958 and travelled to Bletchley. Here we took the branch train through Verney Junction as far as

Brackley (LNWR) station. I had to persuade Harry to climb the hill through Brackley to the GCR station and was able to do so with the promise of lunch. This was quickly served on the ex-Marylebone express between Brackley and Leicester Central. Another walk took us to Leicester (London Road), where we joined the through train from Birmingham (New Street) to Yarmouth (Beach). A dining car was coupled to the rear of the train in Leicester and we stayed in this to South Lynn via the Midland and Midland & Great Northern Joint Line through Bourne and Spalding. The coach rocked so badly over the fens through a station known as Twenty (after the drain) that the attendant put layers of paper on the table-cloth to soak up the tea that vibrated out of the cups. The push-and-pull shuttle took us to King's Lynn, where we boarded the express to Liverpool Street. A good day out!

I hope you will enjoy this next group of pictures, which start at Wootton Bassett in Wiltshire and end at Dalston in Cumbria.

Wootton Bassett, Wiltshire; Class 47, South Wales-Paddington express (1A45), 25 March 1971.
At the turn of the 20th century the railways were in their prime and major construction works were the order of the day. Until then trains through Swindon had gone west to Bath and Bristol, but then it was decided to bore the tunnel under the River Severn and provide a direct route to South Wales terminating at Fishguard with the steamers to Eire. This diverged from the old main line at Wootton Basset, which thus became an important junction. Such trains as 'The Pembroke Coast Express' ran this way to Milford Haven, Neyland and Pembroke Dock, which hitherto had been relatively insignificant. Resorts like Tenby were put on the tourist trail. *2136*

Above Standish Junction, Gloucestershire; Class 45, North-West Country express (1V57), 16 March 1974.

With semaphore signalling it is easy to judge in advance which way a train is going at a junction, but colour lights cannot be so identified from the rear. A train from Swindon has approached the junction behind us and has come to a stand. On the face of it there was plenty of time for it to cross the junction before the express appeared, but it was held for more than 5 minutes. Until quite recent years there had been four tracks from here to Gloucester and the rivalry between the Midland and Great Western is legendary. Obviously such prejudice was still lingering on! *2238*

Below Sandford, Oxfordshire; Class 52, Paddington-Birmingham express (1M11), 26 October 1974.

I'm standing at the site of the former signal box between Didcot and Oxford. A special chartered by the Swindon Co-operative Society to Blackpool for the Illuminations has just gone past and after this express came the Great Western Society's special, with two gleaming steam

locomotives bound for Hereford. This 10-mile stretch of track is probably as much used today as it has ever been, with trains from Birmingham and Worcester and originating services frequently from Oxford in competition with the coaches on the M40. The SRA in its wisdom saw fit to discontinue the innovatory service from Oxford to Swindon last year; it seems that new ideas are not to be encouraged. *2369*

Above right Wolvercot Junction, Oxford; DMU, LCGB special from Witney, winter 1970.

Try as I may, I cannot find a date for this tour, which you have seen already at Welford Park (page 18). The signal box has gone and now a 'ladder'-type junction links the Worcester line on the left with the main line from Birmingham. The Fletton brick building was a sign of things to come. It was quite common to route the trains from Fairford into the loop in the foreground (service discontinued in 1962), and even more so on the down side on the outward run. *2375*

Right Tackley, Oxfordshire; Inter-City units, Birmingham-Paddington express, a Sunday in August 1973.

I'm waiting in this field in sight of the Oxford Canal to see two steam trains run south, the first with *Green Arrow* and the second with *Flying Scotsman*. At the time I thought little of this picture, but today it probably has more historical significance than the others. I once hired one of these units to take the 'Talking of Trains' class from Clapham Junction to Derby calling at Harrow on the Hill, Quainton Road and Clipston & Oxenden, not knowing that special drivers were allocated to them. It so happened that day – and I had not been warned of this – that Trent signal box was being commissioned, so there was substantial delay to services. We were held even longer at Derby for the return, awaiting a special driver from Reading! The line in the picture has been used recently for trial runs of a 'Pendolino', perhaps because Richard Branson lives in the area. *2670*

Oxenden Tunnel, Northamptonshire; Class 47, Glasgow Central-Euston sleeper via Settle & Carlisle, 28 April 1972.
I was told that this train was diverted from the Midland main line at Market Harborough so that the sheets could be sent readily to the laundry at Stonebridge Park. Certainly it was an unusual route, following the slow track of the West Coast Main Line from Roade, and arrival in London was relatively late. No doubt it contributed to the demise of real trains through Settle! The lines are parting company for the tunnels and the signals at the level crossing at Clipston & Oxenden are anticipated by a distant on a gallows' framework. I had been speaking at a conference in Market Harborough, stayed overnight and advised the waitress that I would be back for breakfast when I had photographed this train! 3870

Above Little Bowden, Leicestershire; Class 25 No 25133, empty DMU from Northampton to maintenance depot at Derby, 7 May 1974.

The Northampton-Market Harborough line lost its local passenger and freight services in 1960 but was retained as double track and used in due course by the sleeper seen in the previous picture. The average photographer would never know when any of the occasional freight trains was due, so it came as a pleasant surprise to me while having a sandwich in a layby on the parallel A508 to see this train making its slow way north across the fields. I quickly put the car in gear and managed to overtake the train before it reached Little Bowden Crossing. What a vintage picture it is! Level crossing gates and an LNWR box, both now swept away, an outmoded United Counties double-decker bus and an old pillar box, as well as the unusual train. *3871*

Left Bingham, Nottinghamshire; DMU, Grantham-Nottingham (Midland), 28 September 1974.

Today some commuter trains from Nottingham turn back here during peak hours, while others go on to Skegness and sometimes originate as far west as Manchester Airport and come via the Potteries. Yet more continue south from Grantham to Peterborough and East Anglia. There is some sort of track tamping machine in the siding. *4242*

Above Little Langford, Wiltshire; DMU, Westbury-Salisbury, 19 August 1972.

The perfect rural scene with cattle in the meadow and a local train: what more is there to say? Details of the line can be found on pages 10-11. *1040*

Below St James Park Halt, Devon; DMU, Exeter-Exmouth, 26 September 1974.

Only the branch trains called here, although it was sited on the main line to Waterloo. Look at all the allotments on the right – presumably for railwaymen in the first instance. *1159*

Above Cowley Bridge Junction, Devon; Class 52, down express (1B25), 26 September 1974.
This location has already been seen on pages 16 and 22, but a view in colour doesn't go amiss! *1807*

Below Eynsham, Oxfordshire; DMU, LCGB special returning from Witney, winter 1970.
We've seen this special at Welford Park (page 18) and at Wolvercot Junction (page 41), so now here it is in colour with a good measure of snow. The guard will shortly alight to open the level crossing gates. *2380*

Above **Dorrington, Salop; DMU, Crewe-Cardiff, 4 August 1972.**
On an absolutely marvellous evening, Caer Caradoc is seen on the left, which I climbed back in 1956. The additional single-car unit to help speed the train is absent once again (see page 29) – the civil servant will not be pleased! *2839*

Below **Onibury, Salop; Class 47, down parcels (4V20), 5 August 1972.**
I'm standing on the footbridge adjacent to the level crossing that adjoined the station platform (closed in 1958), but this has now gone and there are automatic lifting barriers. The line speed now is 90mph. *2890*

Above Blaenau Ffestiniog, Gwent; DMU from Llandudno,
29 May 1970.
There is a possibility that much of this surplus slate will be transported elsewhere by rail for road construction purposes, but it seems to take a long time to decide. The road heads over the Crimea Pass to come down near Roman Bridge station on the other side of the mountain. *3685*

Below Bootle, Cumbria; Class 31, up engineer's train,
21 September 1974.
This is a favourite part of the country for me – I never tire of the West Cumbrian coast and the twisting, turning main road to get there. This train came as a complete surprise. *9603*

Above right Batty Wood, Stainforth, North Yorkshire; Class 45, down 'Thames Clyde Express, 3 June 1973.**
In the Ribble Valley, the train is climbing the 'Long Drag' from Settle to Ribblehead. It's a Sunday and to my surprise the train is on time. *8693*

Right Thurston, Suffolk; Class 31, Harwich-Peterborough (1B13), date uncertain.
The co-acting signals are to assist sighting under the bridge on which I am standing. The station here survived the Beeching closures probably because it served the home village of the Minister of Transport at the time. *5672*

Below Swineshead, Lincolnshire; two Class 25s, Nottingham-Skegness (1E86), 19 August 1972.

A picture that is full of detail: the whistle sign, platform signs old and new, lifting barriers and an old telephone box, no doubt threatened by BT's new criteria. When I worked for the RDCA I administered a 'Rural Allocation of Kiosks' scheme whereby the then Post Office authorities would provide such a facility on our recommendation provided that the kiosk took £150 per annum. Such schemes went by the board when Rural and Urban Councils were combined, but until now I had not heard of them being threatened. 6003

Bottom Forth Bridge, Lothian; Class 47, Aberdeen-Edinburgh, September 1974.

What a remarkable structure this is, and look how it dwarfs the cottages below. When I first travelled over it the custom was to throw a penny from the carriage window in the interest of good luck. Presumably the lengthman benefited. Now you can't normally open the window so his salary must have dwindled. 10308

Right Wester Lovat, Highland; Class 26, Kyle of Lochalsh-Inverness, 19 April 1973.

We are looking the other way from the photograph on page 114. Note the ominous snow on the highlands, and that the engine carries a miniature snowplough. 10928

Below right Loch Sqamhaim, Highland; Class 40, Kyle of Lochalsh-Aberdeen, 23 April 1973.

The newspaper-sponsored excursion seen on page 118 is returning home. 11005

Above Loch Dughaill, Highland; Class 25, Kyle of Lochalsh-Inverness, 21 April 1973.
We are very close to Balnacra (see pages 6 and 119), but now looking east. The sky and its reflection in the loch is forever changing and this time a rainbow follows a heavy shower. *11023*

Below Beasdale, Highland; Class 26, Mallaig-Fort William, 7 June 1973.
This is one of the wettest pictures I have ever taken, but I'm glad I did for the Highlands are not always bathed in sunlight as the tourist guides would suggest. I squelched my way from the halt to this location and back again afterwards and ruined a pair of shoes. *11410*

Above Whisker Hill, Retford, Nottinghamshire; Class 47, coal train (6F46) from Yorkshire coalfield to Cottam power station, 21 June 1974.

This layout dates from the days after the Second World War when coal-fired power stations were being sited at intervals along the Trent. The newly nationalised electricity and rail industries combined to relieve the East Coast Main Line of the flat junctions north and south of Retford station by a direct underpass. I can recall joining a Summer Saturday steam train from Sheffield here before that innovation, which had wound its slow way across the main line prior to departure for Skegness via the bridge over the Trent at Torksey (where it had to travel 'wrong line' for structural reasons) and Sykes Junction to Lincoln and Tumby Woodside. *4342*

Below Sharnbrook, Bedfordshire; Class 45, Sheffield-St Pancras express, 30 March 1974.

Some pictures on the Midland now follow, beginning with one taken on the 'Talking of Trains' coach tour that later reached Aynho Junction. The slow lines on the far side of the picture take a route avoiding the summit and pass through a tunnel, which used to help the steam engines on the many freight trains. Today it is a single line with reversible working used regularly on weekdays by the 6.39am from Matlock to St Pancras, which is thus overtaken by the 6.14 ex-Leeds, 7.05 ex-Sheffield, 6.37 ex-Manchester and 7.54 ex-Derby! Sunday trains use the route before midday. *4869*

Above Glendon South Junction, Northamptonshire; Class 45, Nottingham (Midland)-St Pancras express via Melton Mowbray, 4 April 1971.

This used to be the point at which Nottingham trains left the main line before they were diverted via Leicester, the section north of Melton Mowbray was designated to test trains, and the bridge over the Trent transferred to road traffic. I well recall travelling on the principal evening express from London, which slowed down south of Kettering station to switch from the main line and made its first stop, where I alighted, at Melton Mowbray, having had an excellent dinner en route. *4890*

Below Manton Junction, Leicestershire (Rutland); Class 45, diverted St Pancras-Glasgow 'Thames-Clyde Express', 4 April 1971.

Here the Midland joins the older Syston & Peterborough Railway (coming in from the left), whose tracks were shared to Melton Mowbray. During the Beeching era a financial arrangement known as the Cooper Brothers' formula – after a firm of accountants that has never looked back and is now housed in premises associated with BR – was applied to the costing of individual routes. I could never get any satisfaction as to how this was varied in the situation here where the Peterborough-Leicester trains used main-line tracks in part and elsewhere did not. Diverted expresses still proceed via Corby at some weekends, but at this junction the Midland has been reduced to a single-track connection with a crossover at the far end of the tunnel above which I am standing. If a southbound freight train stands at the signal guarding the crossover, it blocks a public right of way!. *4908*

Above Ashwell, Leicestershire; Class 31, Norwich-Birmingham
(New Street), 16 April 1974.

The Syston & Peterborough Railway, as it was originally called, has become a major cross-country artery following the demise of the Midland & Great Northern route and the line from Peterborough to Rugby. As part of the through route to the Midlands from the port of Felixstowe, it is being upgraded here and there as I write. DMUS now run the service illustrated and link various other places, such as Stansted Airport, to the north. Growth in traffic is the order of the day! In the meantime do notice the vintage signs. *4914*

Below Ashwell, Leicestershire; two Class 20s, up freight,
16 April 1974.

It was such a lovely sunny morning that I was reluctant to leave and stood back from the line to take another train in a more rural setting. The station here closed in 1966. I'm on my way home to Kingston-upon-Thames from Giggleswick – not exactly the straightest route. *4916*

Melton Mowbray, Leicestershire; DMU, Birmingham (New Street)-Norwich, 19 May 1974.
Today this is still a real railway station and has some old-world charm both in its façade and the awnings over the platforms and the vintage footbridge. While main-line trains between London and Nottingham no longer come this way, there is a greater diversification of destinations than ever before. Midland Mainline trains are diverted this way sometimes via Corby but do not call. 4927

Right Barber Booth (Edale), Derbyshire;
Class 45, Glasgow (Central)-Nottingham
(Midland) (right), Class 40, westbound
cement train (left), 31 August 1973.
By the time of this picture the proposed
closure of the Settle & Carlisle route was in
place and express trains originated at
Nottingham instead of St Pancras and were
routed by the Hope Valley to the West Coast
over Shap. The scenery and lighting is superb.
5193

Below Barber Booth (Edale), Derbyshire; two Class 25s,
Manchester-Yarmouth Summer Saturday train (1E24),
1 September 1973.
In the distance is Gowhole Tunnel, the western entrance to the Hope
Valley. The second Beeching Report examined duplicate routes and
recommended the retention and development of the Woodhead route
between Sheffield and Manchester and the closure of this line. In the
event BR had to retain the local stations here – now much used by
hikers – and thus closed the more northerly route. During the recent
upgrading of the West Coast Main Line a special service was run this
way between St Pancras and Manchester (Piccadilly) using the south
curve at Dore to avoid Sheffield. *5195*

Left Huddersfield, Springwood Tunnel, West Yorkshire; Class 45, Newcastle (Central)-Liverpool (Lime Street) (1M67), 18 November 1972.
Today each tunnel contains only a single line, the one on the right being reversible for the benefit of trains to Penistone and Barnsley/ Sheffield diverging at Springwood Junction (lower right). The building in the background is used for making musical instruments and maintaining church organs. *4637*

Below left Paddock (Huddersfield), West Yorkshire; DMU to Sheffield, 18 November 1972.
This picture has all the feel of the old North – back-to-back houses mixed with factory premises and a railway viaduct thrown in – and dates from before the line was reduced to single track. I'm pretty certain that the unit will run direct to Sheffield (Midland) via Thurgoland, the disused Victoria station and reversal prior to Nunnery Main Line Junction (rather than Barnsley as today), but cannot verify this fact. *4532*

Above right Horsforth, West Yorkshire; DMU, Leeds-Harrogate, 10 May 1974.
For the capital city of the North, Leeds has few suburban stations, but this is one of them and it seems to be well used. Even the trains to York via Knaresborough come this way now, but electrification has not arrived as in the nearby Aire Valley where the intermediate stations to Shipley have all gone. What a muddle we have made of our railway network! *6980*

Below Wescoe Hill Tunnel, North Yorkshire; Class 31 No 5656, morning King's Cross-Harrogate express, late May 1973.
In the far distance is the viaduct over the River Wharfe that has brought the train out of West Yorkshire. Until 1967 express trains came this way from Leeds to Ripon, Northallerton and beyond, and it is difficult to understand why the line north of Harrogate was closed and services diverted by way of York. Trains are said to be late more often today than hitherto and one reason for this must be the concentration of different journeys on to a limited number of routes with consequent congestion. *6971*

Above **Apperley Junction, West Yorkshire; Class 31 No 31189, westbound breakdown train, 10 May 1974.**
The junction is for Ilkley (and Skipton until 1965 – another contribution to road congestion in Leeds during peak hours). The train is heading for Stainforth, just north of Settle, where a lorry has gone through the parapet of a bridge and is hanging over the tracks. The up 'Thames-Clyde Express' was stopped just north of the accident and had to return nearly 70 miles to Carlisle to set out south again via Shap. *8251*

Left **Ilkley, West Yorkshire; DMU to Leeds, 10 May 1974.**
A thriving country town with considerable commuter traffic with Leeds, its station is next to the shopping centre. Although the track layout has been reduced since the loss of services to Skipton and Otley, electrification has taken place and trains run quickly and frequently to both Leeds and Bradford (Forster Square). *8271*

Left **Hellifield, North Yorkshire; Class 45, up express (1M82), 10 September 1971.**
I'm on my way to Giggleswick once more and pause east of the station to see a train around teatime. I had expected a freight, but as so often it did not materialise! *8417*

Above Newsholme, North Yorkshire; Class 47, Manchester (Victoria)-Glasgow (Central) (1S45), 12 September 1971.
The train has been diverted from the West Coast Main Line on a Sunday and has come via Entwhistle. I have been permitted to trespass on farmland in return for photographing the farmer's daughter! He never even acknowledged the print. Accordingly I'm beside the Blackburn/Hellifield line north of Clitheroe where even today few trains run regularly and the bridges over the main road have not been painted to my knowledge for 40 years. Passengers looking out of the far windows have a glorious view of the River Ribble. *8381*

Below Newsholme, North Yorkshire; two Class 50s, Glasgow Central-Euston express diverted via Settle & Carlisle, 12 September 1971.
Looking north now at much the same location as the last picture, I had been allowed on to the farmland and spent much of the day there. *8380*

Above Long Preston, North Yorkshire; Class 45, Glasgow Central-Nottingham (Midland) (1M86), 12 July 1974.

The train has been checked on the approach to Hellifield and has just been given the right away – hence the exhaust. Steam engines often took water here from a tanker parked on an overbridge by the station; I wonder what the Health & Safety people say about this. The 'M' in the destination indicator refers to a destination in the Midland Region. *8450*

Below South of Settle Junction, North Yorkshire; Class 47, up relief to Eastern Region (1E49), 13 July 1974.

Just behind me is an LMS colour light distant for the junction, set at two levels to delineate the branch and the main line. In later years I was able to photograph this with the farm-owner's consent, but on this occasion it was sadly out of bounds. It is now replaced with a standard colour light. *8453*

Above **Giggleswick, Close Farm, North Yorkshire; DMU, Leeds-Morecambe, 31 May 1973.**
I've used a longer lens for a change – do notice that the train still contains First Class accommodation. The Settle Bypass now runs parallel with the railway just the further side of the train.*8519*

Below **Blaithwaite, North Yorkshire; Class 25, Heysham-Leeds parcels (presumably via Bare Lane-Hest Bank curve), 22 May 1972.**
Ingleborough dominates the horizon to the north. This line – from Settle Junction to Carnforth – still retains double track but is a single long section, the signal box at Wennington remaining switched out, so trains can run only at about 45-minute intervals. As there are so few this hardly matters, but why the first originates at Skipton at 05.43 I shall never understand. It must be a positioning run, but why not stable it at Lancaster overnight? Perhaps someone will explain. Incidentally there is still a crew change at Skipton on Leeds-Carlisle trains as though the division there of Midland and Eastern Regions still survives privatisation. At least it means the buffet is safe! *8529*

Above left **Waterscale, North Yorkshire; DMU, Leeds-Morecambe, 23 September 1972.**
I have nothing particular to say about this picture except that I am en route to see steam between Carnforth and Barrow-in-Furness. 8576

Left **Carnforth, Lancashire; Class 25, Leeds-Heysham parcels, 16 May 1970.**
Until recent years there was a triangular junction here so that trains from Wennington could proceed either into the station – as in the picture – or bypass it and head for Barrow-in-Furness. This spur could have permitted through trains for tourists (say one each way daily) between York and the southern Lake District, which otherwise is difficult of access. But no, the track was lifted. I deliberately used to charter trains to run over this spur, and every time the passage was slow and halting and watched by gangs of men for some reason. 8628

Top **Settle, North Yorkshire; Class 47, Long Meg-Widnes anhydrite, 13 July 1974.**
And so to the Settle & Carlisle in the early 1970s, beginning with a view north of the junction showing the older line to Lancaster bearing away above the train. The Settle Bypass now runs parallel with the older line and some of the woodland has been felled to make way for it. 8638

Above **Langcliffe, North Yorkshire; Class 45 No 45026, down 'Thames Clyde Express' (1S68), date unknown.**
This was the principal train of the day linking London and Scotland via Leeds. Note the stone walls on the boundary – typical of this part of the country. 8678

Above Newhouses, North Yorkshire; Class 40, up freight, 12 October 1973.
We are just north of Horton-in-Ribblesdale and in the open country near the head of the Ribble Valley. 8726

Below Shaw House, North Yorkshire; Class 45, Glasgow-Nottingham (Midland) (1M86), 13 May 1974.
The stone walls now proliferate and act as protection against swirling snow hereabouts, though winters have been kinder of late. 8742

Ribblehead, North Yorkshire; Class 45, St Pancras-Glasgow express, 22 May 1972.
Penyghent dominates the skyline to the south as the express hurries on its way before the formation was reduced to a single track across the viaduct.
The glistening roadway suggests that there has been rain lately. 8779

Above left Garsdale, Cumbria; Class 45, down express, 3 October 1970.
This bleak outpost was the junction for passengers for Northallerton until 1954 and Hawes until 1959. The Wensleydale Railway Company hope to restore the link in due course. 8948

Left Shotlock Hill, North Yorkshire; Class 50, up parcels (5J42), 22 May 1972.
The tunnel mouth is beneath my feet, and since privatisation and restoration of the line much engineering work has been taking place here. There is a construction site on top of the tunnel with most work concentrated to the south. Note how the telephone wires pass above the hill. 8954AQ

Top Shotlock Hill, North Yorkshire; Class 45, up freight (8E15), 3 October 1970.
Wild Boar Fell marks the western edge of the horizon – wonderful contrasting shades. 8954AR

Above right Cumwhinton, Cumbria; Class 45, up 'Thames Clyde Express', 31 August 1974.
The last photo of the S&C is well north and on the outskirts of Carlisle. The station closed in 1956, and since this picture was taken the building, in private hands, has been restored and is a joy to see. 9168

Above Woodhouse (near former Hincaster Junction), Cumbria;
Class 40, Glasgow-Blackpool Easter Saturday express, 13 April
1974.
The West Coast Main Line is newly electrified but an odd train like
this remains diesel-hauled. Trains used to diverge at this point to
Arnside and the Furness area; most of them used the main line only
from Tebay, to which they came from the north-east via Barnard
Castle. 9318

Below Grange Marsh (opposite Arnside), Cumbria; Class 50
No 402, Euston-Barrow-in-Furness express, 25 May 1972.
Along the Kent estuary the railway is elevated above the river on a
causeway that stretches from here to beyond Kent's Bank. It is widened
at the site of Grange station and promenade and there is access across
the line to Holme Island. 9465

Green Road, Cumbria; DMU, Barrow-in-Furness-Carlisle (*above*) and Class 25, up freight (*below*), 25 May 1972.

The station is at the middle left of the picture. One ambition – unfulfilled – was to join the former Whitehaven sleeper at Euston and ask the attendant to wake me in time to alight here. The stock used to run empty back to Barrow and start its night journey to London from there. It really is a remote spot and lonely tracks lead down to the Duddon estuary. Someone locally must commute – there is always a bicycle chained up at the station. When the road crossing was modernised the gates were removed and used on a nearby farm. 9561/9564

Above St Bees, Cumbria; DMU, Sellafield-Workington, 25 May 1972.

There used to be several unadvertised trains for the workers at Sellafield and others for those from the Barrow shipyards, longer than the usual one or two coaches. There is a public school here and it has always seemed to me to be the perfect place for those who want to 'lose' their children to send them. The northern Lake District fells mark the horizon. 9650

Below Aspatria, Cumbria; DMU, Carlisle-Whitehaven, 25 May 1972.

This station has listed building status and is now very smart compared to this view, though its signal box and signals have gone. Today it is said to be the largest population to have a station where trains only stop on request. 9687

Above Waverton, Cumbria; Class 40, down freight, 25 May 1972.
The Maryport & Carlisle line has limited clearance under the bridges, and until the advent of automatic doors and fanlights all passenger stock had bars on the windows. *9691*

Below Dalston, Cumbria; DMU, Whitehaven-Carlisle, 25 May 1972.
The oil terminal here is served by a weekday train that comes from the Carlisle direction and calls between 6am and 8am. It is a useful station to use for park-and-ride purposes for the city. *9693*

4.

THE EAST

My first journey from Liverpool Street was in 1951 when, as a new National Service airman, I made my way to RAF Honington. This involved a change at Mark's Tey and another at Long Melford before arrival at Bury St Edmunds and a bus ride to the camp. What an interesting itinerary it proved to be. The locomotives were vintage and the coaches seemed even older, though comfy and warm. We seemed to amble along through delightful countryside and, although time did not seem to be the first priority, we nonetheless arrived punctually and there was no anxiety about connections. On reflection I feel that the same arrangements had been followed for years and had become second nature to the staff. Bank Holiday Mondays brought change with a through train from Bury to London at 5.49pm, necessitating reversal at Mark's Tey. We used this on one of our circular tours, but I cannot find the details.

One of the signal boxes that I visit regularly is at Shippea Hill between Ely and Thetford. For years it was propped up with sleepers at an angle to avoid it falling into the fen, but it has been rebuilt properly at last and boasts double-glazing (really necessary here to protect against the elements), a Baby Belling, microwave oven, quality heating and a real toilet. Privatisation does seem to have made a difference for the better. But the signalman still has to brave the weather to open the level-crossing gates.

At the signal box known as Deeping St James (near the village of St James Deeping) between Peterborough and Spalding there are also gates to be opened, but now sees at least one northbound freight train mid-afternoon – the 12.37 Felixstowe to Healey Mills carrying paper in Cargowaggons behind an EWS Class 66 locomotive. This must cross the East Coast Main Line on the level when coming off the track from March to gain Werrington Junction and the track towards Lincoln. If such traffic increases congestion will occur; I cannot see a Barkston solution this time. Last year there was an occasion when

the weekend sleeper from Euston to Scotland actually came this way due to engineering work at various points along its route.

Until October 1970 it was possible to travel by express from King's Cross to Peterborough, then direct through Spalding, Boston and Louth to Grimsby by the East Lincs Line. It ran straight across the fen and in part is now converted to a highway (of sub-standard width). Skegness traffic came this way (and still does in part north of Boston), but other coastal resorts such as Sutton-on-Sea and Mablethorpe were reached from a country junction at Willoughby in Lincolnshire. The single-track branch (which had its own bay at the junction) saw Summer Saturday through trains to and from the East Midlands.

There used to be a crossroads of services at Market Weighton, then in the East Riding of Yorkshire, until it closed in 1965. Trains from York to Hull mingled with those from Selby to Driffield. On 3 August 1963 Harry, Alan and I took the through train from Reading West to Rotherham Central and sat in the dining car all the way. We spent the night in Selby so that on the Sunday we could take a DMU excursion (Leeds-Market Weighton-Scarborough-Whitby) to Grosmont. By this time few trains ran east of Selby, and sitting at the back of the unit I recall the masses of dust and leaves that were thrown into the air with our passing. We then went to Middlesbrough via Battersby and to Saltburn before heading for Darlington and Whitley Bay. The second night was spent in Newcastle, and on Easter Monday we went through West Hartlepool and Wetherby to Leeds. In those days the Spen Valley Line was available as an alternative route to Huddersfield, so we took a train that followed this through its many tunnels and steep gradients. To Penistone next and finally Retford, from where we hurried home to King's Cross. What an itinerary, and pure enjoyment!

The Wansbeck Valley Line was another favourite of mine to Rothbury (closed to passengers in 1952 and goods in 1963) and Reedsmouth (closed 1956/1963) with the goods running along the Border Counties Railway to Bellingham. This survived mainly for army purposes as far as Woodburn until 1966. I took a BBC tape recorder on my first visit and travelled on both goods trains but had great difficulty in understanding the broad Geordie accent of the guard. He must have got fed up with my 'pardon?' Another man with a very quiet Northumbrian voice explained how they had to chase sheep off the line regularly, and what had to be done with snowdrifts. A woman with a strong Irish accent sent her churns from Brinkburn to Rothbury for water supplies – quite a range of backgrounds in a small area. While driving to the viaduct at Fontburn when chasing a special passenger train, Trevor Owen explained to me how essential it was to keep the wheels of his Ford car straight when passing over a cattle grid at 60mph! I rejoined the same train at Rothbury later that evening and had the experience of being fly-shunted in a dining car to enable the locomotives to run round the coaches. Watching the engine being spun on the turntable there on my first visit was an education; the table was barely large enough to handle it.

Fambridge, Essex; DMU, Wickford-Southminster, date uncertain.
This branch has since been electrified and has regular through trains to and from Liverpool Street. There is basically an hourly service,

Wooler was another place I enjoyed visiting. On my first trip we came by the goods from Tweedmouth via Sprouston (the last station in the Eastern Region). But then another time I stumbled upon the train entering Wooler and was able to pursue it back to Velvet Hall in the car.

In order to cover the rest of the M&GN before closure in 1959 we travelled from Liverpool Street via Ipswich to Norwich on 4 August 1958. We walked across to the City station, terminus of the branch from Melton Constable, and made our first journey on a DMU, which crossed another at Whitwell & Reepham, later to be the terminus of our first General Manager's Saloon charter tours. We changed at Wisbech North where our express was followed by a so-called stopping train, although all the intermediate stations west of there had already been closed, so it was a bit of a farce! Because we had time in hand before going home we made another circuit from Peterborough outward via Stamford and Morcott, returning via King's Cliffe and Wansford. Happy days.

I hope you will enjoy the following illustrations, which start at Fambridge in Essex and end near Embleton in Northumberland.

although the 11.33 from London terminates at Wickford on a Thursday and the 1.23pm from Southminster doesn't run that day so as to provide a path over the single line for the nuclear flask train. 5622

Above Cressing, Essex; DMU, Witham-Braintree, date uncertain.
This picture was taken the same day as the previous one but is on Agfa film with no indication of date – the diary is silent too. Again the line has since been modernised with electric trains to and from Liverpool Street on an hourly basis. The residents of Braintree were determined not to lose their railway under the Beeching cuts; they didn't give up and now have an enhanced service and high house prices. 5637

Below Ipswich, Suffolk; Class 31, Harwich-Blackpool North, 6 September 1974.
The announcer had a marathon task in giving the names of all the stations served en route – by the time he reached Poulton-le-Fylde he was almost hoarse! This sort of service has now been taken over by two-coach DMUs, and there are a number of these in the sidings awaiting duties to Lowestoft and Cambridge. At the time of writing the tunnel at the far end of the picture has been closed for the track to be lowered to permit larger containers from Felixstowe. During the six weeks involved, freight trains, for example those to Cardiff, have been travelling by way of Dullingham and I have been busy recording these diversions with my camera. 5664

Ely, Ouse River Bridge, Cambridgeshire; Class 37 No 6744, afternoon Peterborough-Harwich train, 18 September 1971.
It was a long walk to reach this location but the weather was set fair and so it proved enjoyable. Do notice the six-wheeled van at the front of the coaches, presumably for parcels traffic. The cathedral can just be glimpsed above the bridge. The signal protects the main line from Cambridge at Ely Dock Junction. 5701

Left Elsenham, Essex; Class 37, Liverpool Street-Cambridge, 9 August 1973.
Now part of the electrified main line from London to King's Lynn, Elsenham was the junction for the light railway to Thaxted until 1952. I never travelled that way so could not enjoy the delights of a halt known as 'Sibley's, for Chickney and Broxted', or the terminus, which the timetable indicated was 'for Great Bardfield (5 miles)'. I wonder if the brickwork in the left foreground marked the platform for the branch. 5562

Below left Littlebury, Essex; Class 31, down express from Liverpool Street, 10 March 1973.
The tunnel in the distance hides the view of the trains from the stately home at Audley End. This valley houses the former A11 road to Norwich, another higher up the hillside to Saffron Walden and, to the right of the railway, the M11 motorway. In connection with the Ipswich Tunnel closure (referred to above) I came to the next bridge north the other day and photographed the special 11.47 Liverpool Street/Norwich via Cambridge and 12.12 equivalent ex-Norwich trains put on for the convenience of through travellers; the electric locos were still attached to the coaches but not taking power. 5567

Above right Harling Road, Norfolk; two Class 25s, Yarmouth-Manchester, 11 August 1973.
It is high summer and a profusion of extra trains are running to and from the East Coast along a line that has seen little modernisation. There are still signal boxes with semaphore signals and level-crossing gates that have to be opened by hand – even in pouring rain – showing how little investment governments have put into railways. The Eastern Region used to hang blue signs along the nearby A11 indicating the presence of the station, which escaped the Beeching cuts and remains open to this day, although with only a meagre stopping service. 5877

Below Bryant's Bridge, Norfolk; two Class 25s, Manchester-Yarmouth Summer Saturday extra, 11 August 1973.
This is the equivalent eastbound service. The Snetterton motor racing circuit is just north of here. 5875

Above left Eccles Heath, Norfolk; Class 40, Norwich-Newcastle express, 15 April 1972.

This train will travel via the joint line from March to Spalding and through Lincoln and Gainsborough to Doncaster on the ECML – very convenient, and running every weekday. Now there are no through trains from the North East and a change is necessary at Peterborough; congestion there is increasing between freight traffic from East Anglia, which, to avoid going northwards up the ECML, has to cross it on the level to gain the line to Spalding, etc. Part of the yard is currently being restored at Whitemoor. How short-sighted were earlier decisions to close the joint line avoiding Peterborough. Our predecessors were not fools. *5874*

Left Eccles Road, Norfolk; Class 25 and unidentified locomotive, Manchester-Yarmouth, 11 August 1973.

There must have been a private siding on the left adjacent to the mill. Although this has been abandoned, another siding behind the train was used in recent years to take in material for widening the A11 trunk road. Because there is only one crossover here and a limitation on the number of wagons that could be moved at one time, the loco took nine of these to Wymondham and returned for the others before bringing the whole consist back west. *5872*

This page Spooner Row, Norfolk; Class 31s, up holiday expresses, 11 August 1973.

I am using a long lens again, and what a charming railway scene with the station in the distance. The road was so quiet that I could enjoy my sandwiches on the bridge parapet, but no longer, as heavy farm traffic now comes this way and has scoured the edges of the carriageway. However, the station and infrastructure remain virtually intact today, although the stopping service is poor. Go and photograph it too! *5863/5862*

Above Reedham Junction, Norfolk; DMU, Norwich-Lowestoft, 9 March 1973.

The train is diverging from the single line ahead to Yarmouth in order to climb above the River Yare by the Reedham swing bridge, which is just around the corner. 5756

Below Aylsham South, Norfolk; Class 31 No 31101, Norwich-Lenwade concrete train, 22 March 1974.

The station closed in 1952, and on a rather misty morning this train is following the horseshoe route from Norwich via Wroxham to the Themelthorpe curve, where the former Great Eastern branch to County School (since lifted) was linked to the former Midland & Great Northern branch from Melton Constable (closed to passengers in 1959). My first outing with the Eastern Region GM's saloon ran to Whitwell & Reepham on 20 July 1974. 5788

Above **Worstead, Norfolk; DMU, Norwich-Sheringham, 9 March 1973.**

Home of the famous cloth, the station buildings have since been replaced on the up side, and the branch has seen some modernisation. A heavy oil tank train passes through here every weekday afternoon on its way from North Walsham to Ipswich. My car is DPB 5J, which dates the view. I can recall joining 'The Broadsman' at Sheringham and travelling in style to Liverpool Street through Worstead with afternoon tea at the start and dinner after Ipswich. Those were the days. 5798

Below **North Walsham, Norfolk; DMU, Sheringham-Norwich, 9 March 1973.**

This station too has been completely rebuilt with a large glass building accommodating passengers bound for the south. It was the junction for Mundesley-on-Sea until 1964, a line operated formerly by the 'GE and Mid & GN Joint', and there was a spur to the M&GN at this point. 5800

Below West Runton, Norfolk; DMU, Sheringham-Norwich, 15 April 1972.
This train will reverse at Cromer where the station has since been modernised as part of a supermarket complex. Trains west of Sheringham came from Melton Constable until 1964; now they run to Holt under the auspices of the North Norfolk Railway. *5812*

Bottom Ely West Curve, Cambridgeshire; Class 40, Newcastle-Norwich (1P16), 8 March 1973.
The signal box that used to stand at Ely North Junction controlled trains from Ely to March, King's Lynn and Norwich respectively. In addition there is this curve, which enables trains to run from March without going into Ely. The 10.43 (SO) Norwich-Peterborough and 3.54pm (SuO) Norwich-Manchester are the only passenger trains currently to use what has become a single line with reversible working. *5917*

Right March, Cambridgeshire; Class 31, holiday train to the coast, 12 August 1972.
Although most of the infrastructure remains, there is an air of dereliction over the right-hand (joint line) platforms today. The tracks there duplicate an alternative route from Whitemoor Junction, which is still in use. *5940*

Below right Whitemoor Junction, Cambridgeshire; Class 31 No 5804, holiday train to the coast (1P20), 12 August 1972.
What an incredible series of curves to bring the train into the joint line platforms at March! The train has come from Spalding and the last coaches are still on the joint line. Meanwhile the train has intersected the Wisbech branch, which runs north behind the sixth coach. In the foreground tracks lead to a triangle between March and Whittlesea; the latter has survived and is being revived as part of Whitemoor marshalling yard, which is being brought back into use. Just out of sight (on the next slide in the collection) is a wonderful gantry of semaphore junction signals. *5949*

Above French Drove & Gedney Hill, Lincolnshire; two Class 25s,
Yarmouth-Manchester, 12 August 1972.

This is an incredibly lonely place in the fens where the roads are such
that the car bounces along if any speed is attempted. I took the 'Talking
of Trains' evening class from Surbiton here by coach and we saw a
DMU pass each way in the early afternoon. We then went on to visit
Ely North Junction box. The station closed in 1961 and the track has
been lifted. 5959

Below Spalding South Junction, Lincolnshire; DMU,
Peterborough-Grimsby, February 1970.

The lines in the foreground (to March) have since gone, while those
on the far side, which linked the Midland & Great Northern route,
went at an earlier date. The main line to Grimsby also ceased to be by
this route in 1970, so that the remaining track forms a loop east of the
ECML from Peterborough to Doncaster and as such has started to take
slow-moving freight from the main line. It was local government that
saved the passenger service, initially just between Peterborough and
Spalding twice a day and subsequently over a greater distance more
frequently. Currently there is just one through working this way – the
11.51 (MF), 12.41 (SO) from Peterborough to Doncaster. 5971

Above Spalding, Lincolnshire; Class 25, up ballast train, February 1970.
Just a shadow of its former self and rather a muddle as seen here, this station serves a local population of at least 20,000. Just look at all the point rodding on the left. *5973*

Below Westhorpe, Lincolnshire; Class 31, Chesterfield-Yarmouth, 12 August 1972.
Just five coaches ran weekly from the Eastern Region boundary station at Chesterfield – more a relief train than anything else. Here we are in the vast fenland between Spalding and Sleaford. *6106*

Above Burton Penwardine, Lincolnshire; Class 47 No 1551, down coal empties (9D86), 12 August 1972.
A few miles further north, we are now quite near Sleaford South Junction and the town's avoiding line to Lincoln. The three-arch bridges are a feature of the line. *6117*

Below Ruskington, Lincolnshire; Class 31, down holiday express (1N24), 12 August 1972.
We are north of Sleaford now. This station closed in 1961 but was rebuilt and opened by Lincolnshire County Council in 1975. Most local trains run between Peterborough and Lincoln. *6130*

Above Digby, Lincolnshire; Class 31, Yarmouth-Chesterfield (1P13), 12 August 1972.
Here is our 'relief' train returning from the coast in the late afternoon (see page 82). *6132*

Below Washingborough, Lincolnshire; Class 37, Manchester-Harwich boat train (1E87), 12 August 1972.
This was the train of the day over the Joint line. I used it in 1952 when on National Service, and while travelling from Bury St Edmunds to a course on leisure in Manchester; at that time the train continued to Liverpool. I recall how it approached Lincoln at a crawl so that the level crossing gates over Pelham Street could be left open to road traffic until the last minute to avoid gridlock in the city – even then! There is a bridge now. At a later date I had breakfast and lunch on the train. You can just make out the cathedral above the bridge. *6133*

Above Stainton-by-Langworth, Lincolnshire; Class 47, Cleethorpes-King's Cross express (1A34), 12 August 1972.
With the closure of the East Lincs Line through Spalding and Boston in 1970, a substitute service was run for a time calling at Market Rasen. Now that has been withdrawn and passengers from Grimsby – if there are any left – are expected to change at Newark. *6173*

Below Beckingham, Nottinghamshire; Class 40, Newcastle (Central)-Norwich, September 1970.
Here is the eastbound working of the train we saw above at Eccles Heath (page 76). The loops have survived and are now equipped with colour lights. The train has a motley set of stock of many colours. *6165*

Above Heckington, Lincolnshire; DMU to Skegness, 21 August 1971.
This period piece of a picture has Great Northern somersault signals, signal box and nameboard, all dominated by the magnificent windmill. This was a day when the line would be heavily used by holiday trains. *5997*

Below Rawson's Bridge (Maud Foster), Boston, Lincolnshire; Class 47, Skegness-King's Cross (1A50), 19 August 1972.
The train is crossing the West Fen Drain, and until 1970 would have headed due south to the ECML at Peterborough, but now it has to run via Grantham, travelling over the Barkston spur, which will be lifted when the new curve is completed at Allington Junction, meaning that trains from the east will enter Grantham from the west! *6015*

Below Sibsey, Lincolnshire; Class 31 No 5835, Skegness-Leeds (1J28), 19 August 1972.
We will now have a sequence of pictures along the former East Lincs Line and Skegness branch. For some reason, presumably the condition of the bridges over the watercourses, the formation was reduced to single track north from Boston as far as Sibsey, and this train is slowing down as it leaves the double track. At the time this station boasted a host of original Great Northern signs. 6020

Bottom Old Leake, Lincolnshire; Class 31 No 5559, southbound holiday train from Skegness, 19 August 1972.
Look at all the concrete tank traps to keep the invading Germans away

from the railway – presumably they would have gone round the end and through the gates! Nevertheless they provided me with useful height in taking the picture, although I had some difficulty scaling the blocks. 6023

Right East Fen Crossing, Lincolnshire; two Class 25s, Skegness-East Midlands (1M35), 19 August 1972.
Because the track here had been kept to main-line standards for the King's Cross-Grimsby expresses and was virtually straight for 15 miles, these holiday trains got up
quite a lick and, running on jointed track, made quite a noise for those inside the coaches and those at the lineside. The line is plagued by level crossings; note the distant signal for the next one north (or the one beyond?), which you can see at Eastville in the distance. The apparatus on the telephone pole (left) to indicate the presence of trains is lit (?) by an oil lamp in a vintage case. There are lots of telephone wires. 6024

Below right Stickney, Lincolnshire; DMU, Skegness-Lincoln, 2 May 1970.
Away from the 'main line' for a moment – we connect with it at Bellwater Junction – we wait quietly on the grass-grown platform (closed in October 1970) for the train to creep in. From time to time on Summer Saturdays the place would be shaken by a passing holiday train from, say, Sheffield via Retford and Torksey. 6040

Above Little Steeping, Lincolnshire; two Class 25s, holiday train from Skegness (1M02), 19 August 1972.

The signal box here had been sinking backwards for years and I wonder whether it is still there. Because of the chaotic manner in which wayside station closures took place, none survive on the former East Lincs Line, yet there is a full complement on the branch to Skegness and between Boston and Grantham. The signal has been restored to danger quickly as there is a procession of trains due. Some coaches are in maroon and others in blue and white. *6043*

Below Thorpe Culvert, Lincolnshire; Class 47 No 1564, King's Cross-Skegness (1D?1), 19 August 1972.

We've turned the corner, as it were, on to the branch. Do notice the archive nameboard, the vintage oil lamp standard and the Great Northern signal behind the train, as well as the level-crossing gates. I believe vast changes may have occurred recently according to the railway press. *6052*

Above **Hensall, North Yorkshire; DMU, Leeds-Goole, 25 May 1974.**
We now move to a new area altogether, the Lancashire & Yorkshire tentacle into the old East Riding of Yorkshire. At nearby Hensall Junction today the endless line of trains turns off to serve Drax power station, but the passenger service is meagre with two trains eastbound and three westbound at present. *6341*

Below **Wressle, Humberside; Trans-Pennine DMU, Hull-Liverpool, October 1973.**
This is another line on which the wayside stations have survived; indeed, the 'Hull Executive' now comes this way rather than via Goole. The communities served are small and it is a delight to drive from station to station. *6355*

Left Howden, Humberside; Trans-Pennine DMU, Liverpool-Hull, October 1973.
Don't get out here unless you have pre-booked a taxi, for the town is on the horizon some distance away. There used to be another station adjacent to the main street on the Hull & Barnsley, but this route has been lifted and houses built over the site. *6356*

Below left Nafferton, Humberside; Class 40, Scarborough-King's Cross via Bridlington express, 16 September 1972.
We are on the Hull-Scarborough line now, which was threatened with closure but was saved in part by the comedian Ken Dodd, who trumpeted its virtues and advertised its possibilities. You can see the capstan in the signal box for opening and closing the gates. There is basically an hourly service between here and Bridlington/Hull with occasional sorties to Scarborough. *6413*

Above right Lowthorpe, Humberside; Class 40 No 349, excursion to Scarborough (1Z23), 16 September 1972.
This station had closed in 1970 and looked pretty derelict when I took this picture. It is on a bend of the line and had staggered platforms either side of the level crossing. *6416*

Below Cayton, North Yorkshire; Class 40 No 272, Scarborough-King's Cross via Bridlington, 16 September 1972.
This station closed as long ago as 1952; it was badly sited for the village and travellers to Scarborough would undoubtedly take the bus. In more recent years the formation has been reduced to a single track between Seamer Junction and Filey and the signals have gone. Do notice the dining car at the front of the train, almost the only one to serve the resort and it only came *from* there; how it got there is a mystery. *6469*

Above Seamer West Junction, North Yorkshire; Class 40 No 267,
Scarborough-Leicester, 16 September 1972.
This train used to call at Filey Holiday Camp, which necessitated the
locomotive running round the train and the retention of a little-used
loop. Do notice the grand signals and the North Eastern Railway
milepost in the grass (left). Until 1950 trains diverged here to the left
on the Forge Valley Line to Pickering. *6471*

Below Knapton, North Yorkshire; DMU, York-Scarborough,
16 September 1971.
This location is marked for miles around by a maltings and is also near
a modern power station, but the station closed in 1930. The signal box
and semaphores too have since disappeared. *6603*

Little Bytham, Lincolnshire; Class 55 'Deltic', down 'Yorkshire Pullman' (*above*), and Class 47, down 'Hull Pullman' (*left*), 14 June 1974.

Back on the East Coast Main Line proper, this is a famous place indeed. It was here that *Mallard* achieved 126mph in 1938, still a world speed record for steam traction. The Pullman cars can clearly be seen towards the back of the 'Yorkshire Pullman' and thus near the barrier at the terminus for latecomers! Not far behind was the Hull train, also with its Pullmans at the rear. 5389/5391

Bottom Swayfield, Lincolnshire; Class 55 'Deltic', up express (1A08), 23 July 1972.

In steam days Stoke Bank, as this stretch of line is called, marked a noticeable slowing of down expresses, but today with electrification it means nothing and more stops can be made at Peterborough without inhibiting speeds. The 'Deltic' has just overhauled a freight train on the up slow line. Do notice the telephone wires. 5396

Above right Swayfield, Lincolnshire; Class 55 'Deltic', down express (1S17), 23 July 1972.

The 'Deltic' is powering up the bank as the goods train seen in the previous photograph disappears into the distance. 5392

Right Swayfield, Lincolnshire; Class 55 'Deltic', up express (1A21), 15 February 1970.

At a totally different time of the year the scene, though sunny, looks distinctly cold. The four tracks become two just north of here to enter Stoke Tunnel at the summit and about 100 miles from London. 5394

Stoke Tunnel (north end), Lincolnshire; Class 55 'Deltic', down express, 3 May 1970.
On the left of the picture are High Dyke Sidings, where ironstone trains used to be concentrated after coming off the branch. It is said that the bridge designed to carry the branch over the widened A1 nearby never saw a train. The main line runs downhill to Grantham. 5397

Above Stoke Tunnel (north end), Lincolnshire; Class 31, up parcels, 3 May 1970.

It's not often that I trespass on railway property – normally I get a permit – but I'm glad that I did so on this occasion for the two pictures are quite memorable archives. 5398

Below Barkston South Junction, Lincolnshire; Class 55 'Deltic', down 'Tees-Tyne Pullman', 23 July 1972.

This junction (behind the train) is to disappear and with it Barkston East box so as to facilitate the operation of more regular GNER trains, particularly a regular half-hourly service between London and Leeds, which has been precluded by the slow Skegness service that currently also uses the main line between Grantham and the junction. Peter Handford, the great recorder of trains, recalls how he spent several nights here before getting a perfect take with a steam-hauled goods train heading out of the loop. 5408

Left Dry Doddington, Lincolnshire; Class 55 'Deltic', up express (1E05), 22 August 1970.
I love the way the bridge in the background leaps from its surroundings. It precedes up and down loops at Claypole. *5417*

Below left Ranskill, Nottinghamshire; Class 47, up express (1E07), 14 June 1974.
Years ago trains from London were often cautioned here if there was trouble ahead in Doncaster. *5436*

Right Ranskill, Nottinghamshire; Class 47, down express (1S33), 14 June 1974.
As trains got quicker so sighting arrangements for signals became more important. Notice how the post supporting this semaphore has been lengthened so that a driver can identify its outline as soon as he passes under the A638 (former A1). *5437*

Below Wylam Junction, Northumberland; Class 40, Newcastle-Largs Summer Saturday train, 6 October 1973.
I was advised at high level that this train only ran to preclude local coach firms from getting a licence to run to the Scottish coast. The tracks that have been lifted ran past George Stephenson's birthplace and entered Newcastle north of the Tyne. *7631*

Above Barhaugh Farm, Cumbria; DMU, Alston-Haltwhistle, 17 June 1972.

This really charming scene is taken from a road that is descending a steep hill with awkward bends. I don't think that the preserved South Tynedale Railway has reached this spot yet, but it must be soon. BR shut the line in 1976, which necessitated the construction of a new road and river bridge near Coanwood. *7705*

Below How Mill, Cumbria; Class 37, eastbound oil tanks, 17 June 1972.

This train is climbing out of the Eden Valley and is making heavy weather of it. Built as long ago as 1832, the line has deep brick-lined cuttings – which this train is approaching – and brick causeways over low land. *7777*

Whinney Hill, near Embleton, Northumberland; Class 47s, down (*above*) and up expresses, 30 August 1974.
We are now back on the East Coast Main Line north of Newcastle, which Dr Beeching wanted to shut but failed because of the local establishment. The clouds behind the down train really threaten something awful! Looking from the other side of the bridge, the up train heads away from the Scottish border at Marshall's Meadows just beyond Berwick-upon-Tweed, which we will visit shortly. *8047*

5.

SCOTLAND

We start our illustrations at the border on the East Coast Main Line just north of Berwick-upon-Tweed, but by far the majority of them are taken on the scenic route between Dingwall and the Kyle of Lochalsh in the days when freight was still carried that way. Mike Esau feels that relatively few pictures have been published of this line.

Before we get there, can I refer to the North Berwick branch, which now has one of the best services it has ever enjoyed connecting it with Edinburgh. Ladies clad in tweed dresses join the train, which has an upper-class feel to it today. Intriguing! While DMUs operate on Saturdays, the branch is electrified and currently four ex-Virgin coaches are pushed and pulled by main-line locomotives. When we ran a special there from Alnmouth we had to be given authority to propel from Drem. In the event our short train had been driven at such speed on the main line (catching up the sleeper and being held by it at Dunbar) that the locomotive caught fire on the branch and had to be replaced in Edinburgh.

Had I done more research when we chartered our Scottish specials I would have taken one of them from Edinburgh to Glasgow via Shotts so that we could call at Addewell and Breich, two jolly rural stations. As it was we covered Oban, Wick and Thurso, Stranraer and other places over the years. To facilitate access to and from the dining car from the saloons for lunch and dinner we had to make pre-arranged stops. I recall that one of these was at Auchinleck and another at Altnabreac in Caithness, a station that served nothing but an empty wilderness. For a lunch call to be made there must have been historical and unlikely to be repeated.

To get an adequate supply of pictures on the line to the north and the one to the Kyle we hired a car from Dingwall some years ago and carried out a lot of reconnaissance. This included racing a train from Kildonan to Kinbrace, taking pictures from the car windows. On my first visit we had travelled by bus from Wick to Thurso; it was a double-decker and I recall that the conductress sat on the sideways bench seat doing her knitting. When we took the saloons to Wick we couldn't understand why there was no water in the toilet tank despite filling at Inverness. It wasn't until we reached Wick that a fitter found that the drain cocks had been left open from stabling through the winter, and soon afterwards we were all right.

It seems appropriate that the last picture should illustrate Mallaig. One Saturday, having come from Skye, I changed at Fort William to the dining car for dinner, then to the sleeper, which I vacated in the night at Newcastle-upon-Tyne, transferring to a room in the Station Hotel. I arrived home the following morning via York.

Opposite above **Marshall's Meadows, Borders; Class 47, up express (1E83), 29 August 1974.**
In the early days of British Railways the East Coast Main Line was divided between three Regions. The Eastern ran from London to Shaftholme Junction (north of Doncaster), the North Eastern from there to this point, and the Scottish Region northwards. Meetings were held regularly to co-ordinate the timing of through trains. As you can see, the line soon runs beside the North Sea. *8103*

Opposite below **Houndwood, Borders; Class 47, down express (1S31), 29 August 1974.**
It was in this area that severe floods in 1948 washed away many of the bridges and damaged the embankments so that through trains were diverted at Tweedmouth (Berwick-upon-Tweed) west to Kelso and to St Boswells on the former 'Waverley Route', by which they reached Edinburgh. *8153*

Above Grantshouse, Borders; Class 47, down express (1S27), 29 August 1974.

Electrification has taken place and today colour lights replace the semaphore signals, but the up and down loops remain in use. *8166*

Below Grantshouse, Borders; Class 40, down replacement express, 27 May 1972.

We were expecting the down 'Flying Scotsman', but instead, and belatedly, this appeared. A derailment had occurred just north of Chathill and a scratch set had been brought into use at Berwick. *8168*

Midcalder Junction, Lothian; Class 45, freightliner from Glasgow area, 31 August 1974.
This line now carries about an hourly service of DMUs between Edinburgh and Glasgow via Shorts. Addewell is one of the most inaccessible stations I know and Breich, at the edge of the Pentlands, only has a few trains serving its small population. But the diverging line in the picture has been electrified and carries regular trains between King's Cross and Glasgow, which complete a flattened horseshoe between here and the city, and to Edinburgh and northwards from the West Coast Main Line. *10085*

Above Harburn, Lothian; Class 25 No 25231, Edinburgh portion of WCML express detached at Carstairs, 31 August 1974.
This station closed in 1966, but as stated above electrification is now in place and many more through expresses use the route on a regular basis. Beyond here the line runs through very uninviting countryside. *10079*

Below Kingsfield, near Linlithgow, Lothian; Class 27 No 27117 and another at the rear, Edinburgh-Glasgow express, 31 August 1974.
It had been the intention for years to speed up this service, particularly after the opening of the M8, and today it takes 50 minutes for the 47-plus miles. In the process sets were run with locos at each end – as in this picture – and at other times push-pull working was employed. Do notice the distant signal. *10140*

Above Dairsie Mains, Fife; DMU, Edinburgh-Dundee, 22 June 1974.
A member of the 'Talking of Trains' class decided that he would like to leave the South East and become a postman at St Andrews. What a good idea! He and his wife invited me to spend weekends with them; this I could do easily by virtue of the King's Cross sleeper, which called at Cupar. The attendant would bring my tea and biscuits by Kirkcaldy, I would lie there with the window open enjoying the fresh Scottish air, and get up in time to be met and take breakfast with my hosts. Perfect! Hence this picture on a Saturday morning. *10355*

Right Dunninald, Tayside; Class 40, up freight, 22 June 1974.
Later on this day *Sir Nigel Gresley* took a special south and just in front of it came this freight. Lunan Bay station (closed to passengers in 1930, and goods in 1964) is nearby. *10557*

Right Ferryden, Tayside; Class 27 No 27039, Aberdeen-Edinburgh local, 22 June 1974.
Before returning to Cupar we rounded off the day by looking across the Montrose Basin. The River South Esk flows into the North Sea here and passes beneath the viaduct in the photograph. Presumably on grounds of economy this carries but a single track from Usan to the south and is the only such section between London and Aberdeen. *10562*

Above Wester Lovat, Highland; Class 25, Inverness-Kyle of Lochalsh, 19 April 1973.

This is the first of a series of pictures taken mainly between Dingwall and the Kyle. They speak for themselves, so I do not intend to add much narrative. This first is on the 'main' line about 6 miles north of Inverness and not far from Lentran station (closed in 1960). The equivalent A9 to the north now bridges the Beauly Firth and runs over the Black Isle in the back of the picture. *10926*

Below Lochluichart, Highland; Class 26, Inverness-Kyle of Lochalsh, 10 April 1971.

Pictures taken on this day are from a car hired at Inverness after travelling north with friends on the 'The Royal Highlander' sleeper, which arrived 2 hours late! *10956*

Right Loch-a-Chuillinn, Highland; Class 26, Inverness-Kyle of Lochalsh, 20 April 1973.
Below right Druimdhu, Highland; Class 25, Inverness-Kyle of Lochalsh, 21 April 1973.

The line snakes through the desolate landscape. *10959/10975*

**Achnasheen, Highland; Class 25, Kyle of Lochalsh-Inverness,
21 April 1973** (*above left*), **and Class 26 No 5337, down freight,
20 April 1973** (*below left*).

I spent a very happy Easter with friends at the Achnasheen Hotel and
my bedroom overlooked the up platform. On most trains the drivers
and guards had a dram here before proceeding on their way; it occupied
the time while the trains crossed on the single line. In the days before
the accountants had too much influence, a dining car ran on the back
of the train from Inverness as far as here and was then exchanged with
the train that returned. What a sensible idea! *10980/10982*

Above **Glen Carron, Highland; Class 25, Kyle of Lochalsh-
Inverness, 20 April 1973.**

In those days parcels and other items were carried in the van that
usually accompanied the passenger coaches. *10995*

Below **Ledgowan, Highland; Class 25, Kyle of Lochalsh-
Inverness, 19 April 1973.**

Note the snow on the tops, though the sheep don't seem to be
bothered. *10999*

Glen Carron, Highland; Class 40, Kyle of Lochalsh-Aberdeen special, 23 April 1973.
An Aberdeen newspaper has sponsored an excursion on Easter Monday. Looks very wild above! 11015

Right Achnashellach, Highland; Class 26, Kyle of Lochalsh-
Inverness, 10 April 1971.
There's a very long footpath north from here through the mountains,
but only for the very hardy and well-equipped. *11021*

Below Balnacra, Highland; Class 26, up freight, 21 April 1973.
Another wild panorama. *11026*

Left Strathcarron, Highland; Class 26, up freight (right), passes down special, 21 April 1973.
As you can see, the crossing of trains is a cause for excitement in this area. Do notice the deer antlers on the platform (bottom right). *11030*

Below Cuddies Point, Highland; Class 26, Inverness-Kyle of Lochalsh, 10 April 1971.
When I first drove to Strome Ferry I had to queue for 3 hours to cross on the small boat. For years now a road has run parallel with the railway south of the loch and turns here to pass over the headland. *11044*

Right Duncraig, Highland; Class 25, Inverness-Kyle of Lochalsh, 9 June 1973.
As you can see it is pouring with rain, but I managed to jump out of the car at the last minute. *11048*

Below right Carn an t-saluinn, Highland; Class 26, Kyle of Lochalsh-Inverness, 10 April 1971.
Better weather! *11058*

Above Kyle of Lochalsh, Highland; Class 26 for Inverness,
10 April 1971.
Before the construction of the controversial road bridge here,
passengers took to the Kyleakin ferry for Skye or stayed at the Lochalsh
Hotel of LMS origin with bedroom doors identical to those in the
Derby Training School. *11075*

Left Kyle of Lochalsh, Highland; 10 April 1971.
Before the road improvements between Garve and Ullapool and the
transfer of the Stornaway ferry to that port, milk churns were normally
transferred from shore to ship on ancient trolleys. *11076*

Above right Invershin, Highland; Class 25, Inverness-
Wick/Thurso, 9 April 1971.
Back to the main line now for two pictures. Readers wanting to know
more about this location should turn to page 93 of *Dawn of the Diesels*
Part 1 (Silver Link Publishing, 1997). *11118*

Right Strathsteven, Highland; Class 25, Inverness-Wick/Thurso,
9 April 1971.
As you can see, they are reconstructing the road to a new bridge over
the railway. *11165*

Above left Crianlarich (Upper), Central; Class 26s, trains to and from Mallaig and Glasgow, 12 April 1971.
We are returning home from our short holiday, having left the hire car at the Kyle and taken the boat from there to Mallaig. The buffet here was notable for business while the trains crossed in the loop. *11259*

Left Glenfinnan Viaduct, Highland; Class 27, Fort William-Mallaig, 6 June 1973.
The weather looks very ominous – and it was! This is the first viaduct to be constructed mainly of concrete and laid the foundations of the McAlpine business. *11355*

Above Glenfinnan, Highland; Class 27, Fort William-Mallaig, 6 June 1973.
When we ran a special with the two GM saloons from the Scottish Region, including our first dining-car, we really wanted to travel from Glasgow to Mallaig and Oban, but time and availability of loops at the right places meant that we had to turn back here to Crianlarich. *11375*

Right Creag Globhar Tunnel; Class 26, Glasgow-Mallaig, 6 June 1973.
This is not an easy location to find or reach, and a lot of climbing is involved. Probably the environment will have closed in on the view by now, but I really don't know. Loch Eilt is in the distance. *11385*

Above Loch Nan Uamh viaduct, Highland; Class 27, Glasgow-Mallaig, 7 June 1973.
At this wonderful location there is little warning of the train's approach and it soon gets lost in the tunnel. It then reappears to wind its way round the north side of the water. *11401*

Below Mallaig, Highland; two Class 27s, LCGB special to Glasgow, 3 June 1972.
The end of the line, and the end of the book! *11437*

INDEX

Roman numerals indicate the colour pages.

Diesel locomotives (TOPS Class Nos)
Class 20 51
Class 25 6, 22, 29, 48, 53, 59, 60, 75, 76, 82, 83, 89, 90, 112, 114, 115, 116, 117, 121, 123, VI, VIII
Class 26 114, 115, 116, 119, 120, 121, 122, 124, 125, 126, VII, VIII
Class 27 112, 113, 124, 125, 127
Class 31 51, 55, 56, 72, 74, 77, 78, 81, 83, 84, 85, 88, 95, 98, 99, 103, IV, V
Class 33 1, 12, 13, 14, 15
Class 35 11, 12, 20, 30, 36
Class 37 32, 34, 73, 74, 85, 97, 106
Class 40 53, 66, 69, 76, 80, 86, 92, 93, 94, 105, 110, 113, 118, VII
Class 45 19, 22, 23, 27, 36, 40, 42, 43, 49, 50, 53, 54, 56, 58, 61, 62, 67, 64, 65, 111, V
Class 47 5, 6, 8, 10, 26, 28, 30, 39, 42, 43, 44, 47, 49, 57, 58, 61, 84, 86, 87, 90, 98, 104, 105, 107, 109, 110, III, VI
Class 50 57, 64, 66
Class 52 19, 23, 31, 40, II
Class 55 100, 101, 102, 103, 104

Diesel multiple units
Diesel-electric 3, 14
Diesel-mechanical 2, 11, 16, 17, 18, 21, 25, 29, 31, 32, 33, 35, 41, 45, 46, 48, 52, 54, 55, 56, 59, 60, 67, 68, 69, 71, 72, 78, 79, 80, 82, 87, 89, 91, 92, 94, 96, 106, 113, I, II, III, IV; 'Inter-City' units 41; Trans-Pennine 91

Locations
Abergavenny 29
Achnasheen 116
Achnashellach 119
Apperley Junction 56
Arnside 66
Ashwell 51
Aspatria 68
Aylsham 78
Aynho Junction 5, 42

Balnacra 119
Barber Booth, Edale 53
Barhaugh Farm, Cumbria 106
Barkston South Junction 103
Bearley 45
Beasdale VIII
Beckingham 86
Bere Ferrers 17
Bicknoller 20
Bingham 48
Blaenau Ffestiniog 35, IV
Blaithwaite 59
Bootle IV
Borthddu 32
Bruern Abbey Crossing 44
Bryant's Bridge 75
Burton Penwardine 84

Calstock 2
Carn an t-saluinn 121
Carnforth 60
Cattal 96
Cayton 93
Chapelton 17
Chepstow 36
Church Stretton 25
Claverdon 46
Coed-y-Uyn 35

Combe St Stephen Viaduct 23
Cowley Bridge Junction 16, 22, II
Creag Globhar Tunnel 125
Cressing 72
Crewkerne Tunnel 13
Crianlarich 124
Cuddies Point 120
Cumwhinton 65

Dairsie Mains, Fife 113
Dalston (Cumbria) 69
Digby 85
Doniford 21
Dorrington III
Druimdhu 115
Dry Doddington (ECML) 104
Duncraig 121
Dunninald, Tayside 113
Dunster 21

East Fen Crossing 89
Eccles Heath (Norfolk) 76
Eccles Road (Norfolk) 76
Edale 54
Elsenham 74
Ely 73; West Curve 80
Embleton 107
Eynsham II

Fambridge 71
Ferryden, Tayside 113
Forth Bridge VI
French Drove & Gedney Hill 82

Garsdale 64
Garth 33
Giggleswick 59
Glen Carron 117, 118
Glendon South Junction 50

Glenfinnan 125; Viaduct 124
Glynneuadd 30
Grantshouse 110
Great Ayton 97
Green Road (Cumbria) 67
Greenwood (ECML) 98

Hammerton 95
Hanging Langford 11
Harburn 112
Harling Road 75
Heckington 87
Hellifield 56
Hensall 91
Heytesbury 12
Hincaster Junction (Woodhouse) 66
Honeybourne West Loop 44
Honiton 14
Horsforth 55
Houndwood 109
How Mill, Cumbria 106
Howden 92
Huddersfield 54
Hurst Green Junction 1

Ilkley 56
Invershin 123
Ipswich 72

Kildale 96
King's Nympton 16
Kingsfield, Linlithgow 112
Kintbury 19
Knapton 94
Knucklas 34
Kyle of Lochalsh line 6, 114-122,
    VIII-VIII; terminus 122

Langcliffe 61
Lealholm 97
Ledgowan 117
Leominster 28
Letchworth 98
Little Bowden 48
Little Bytham 100
Little Langford I
Little Steeping 90
Littlebury 74

Llangunllo 34
Llanwrtyd 33
Loch-a-Chuillinn 115
Loch Nan Uamh viaduct (Mallaig
    line) 126
Lochluichart 114
Long Preston 58
Lowthorpe 93
Ludford 27
Ludlow 26

Mallaig 126
Manton Junction 50
March 81
Marshall's Meadows 109
Meldreth & Melbourn 99
Melton Mowbray 52
Midcalder Junction 111

Nafferton 92
Nant-y-Derry 29
Newbury 18
Newhouses 62
Newsholme 57
North Walsham 79
Norton Bavant 12

Old Leake 88
Onibury III
Orleton 27
Oxenden Tunnel 47

Pinhoe 15

Ranskill 104-105
Rawson's Bridge 87
Reedham Junction 78
Retford 49
Ribblehead 67
Ruskington 84

St Bees 68
St James Park Halt (Exeter) I
Sandford 40
Seamer West Junction 94
Settle 61
Settle Junction 58
Sharnbrook 49

Shaw House 62
Shotlock Hill 64-65
Sibsey 88
Spalding 83; South Junction 82
Spooner Row 77
Stainforth V
Stainton-by-Langworth 86
Standish Junction 40
Stanway Viaduct 43
Stickney 89
Stoke Tunnel 102-103
Strathcarron 120
Strathsteven 123
Sugar Loaf summit 32
Swayfield (ECML) 100-101
Swineshead VI

Tackley 41
Talaton 14
Teignmouth 23
Templeton 31
Thorpe Culvert 90
Thurston V
Toddington 42
Tregroes Moor 31

Washingborough 85
Waterscale 60
Waverton 69
Welford Park 18
Wescoe Hill Tunnel 55
West Runton 80
Wester Lovat 114
Westhorpe 83
Whitemoor Junction 81
Willersey 6, 43
Wilton 10
Witham 19
Wolf's Castle 30
Wolvercot Junction 41
Wood End 45
Woolston 3
Wootton Bassett 39
Worstead 79
Wrenbury 8
Wressle 91
Wylam Junction 105
Wylye 11